delish

INSANE SWEETS

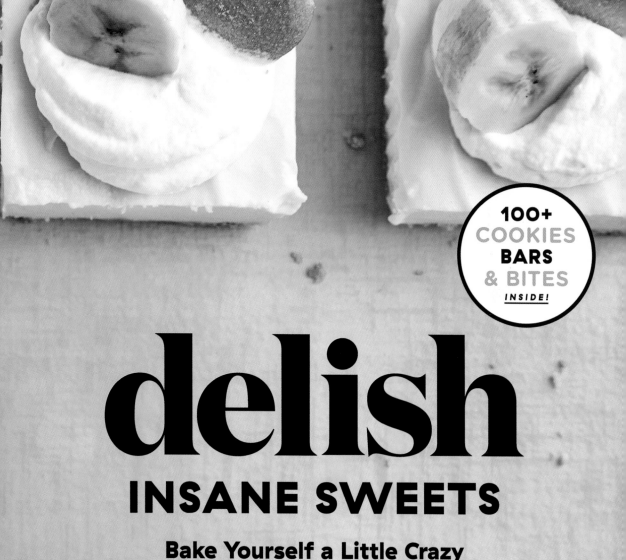

delish

INSANE SWEETS

Bake Yourself a Little Crazy

Joanna Saltz & the Editors of Delish

HOUGHTON MIFFLIN HARCOURT
BOSTON   NEW YORK

For information about permission to
reproduce selections from this book, write
to trade.permissions@hmhco.com or to
Permissions, Houghton Mifflin Harcourt
Publishing Company, 3 Park Avenue,
19th Floor, New York, New York 10016.

hmhbooks.com

*Library of Congress Cataloging-in-
Publication Data is available.*

ISBN 978-0-358-19334-0
ISBN 978-0-358-19303-6 (ebk)

Endpaper illustrations © Dn Br / MicroOne
AVIcon / Fireofheart / Shutterstock

Printed in China

SCP 10 9 8 7 6 5 4 3 2
4500779994

TO THE PEOPLE
WHO ALWAYS
HAVE ROOM FOR
DESSERT

CONTENTS

INTRODUCTION

I USED TO BE AN extremely salty person. I would choose sour cream and onion potato chips over brownies any day of the week. I'd be one of those people who would happily order a cheese plate after dinner. I never really loved sweet things.

And then Delish happened.

Since we launched four and a half years ago, the Delish team has spent hundreds of combined hours a week producing thousands upon thousands of recipes and videos—all in the name of making people feel as comfortable cooking as they do eating. And SO MANY of those man-hours were tied up in testing and retesting desserts: cookies, brownies, cakes, etc. The treats would come out of the kitchen, begging to be tried. And at some point over the years, it became useless to turn it all down. Now I get a straight-up headache if I haven't had two brownies by three p.m.

It should go without saying that the recipes in this book are some of the best treats we've ever made. And I honestly believe it's because they were created by some of the sweetest people in the food industry—a team of editors who care about each other as much as they do about their work. These are people who pack up left-overs for one another or go out of their way to make super-niche treats on someone's birthday (read some of their sweet stories that follow)—they're not normal.

So whether you're making something for a heartbroken friend, an office birthday, or a school bake sale, trust that everything on these pages are the kinds of bites built to instantly make people feel better. Even the saltiest of people won't be able to resist.

JOANNA SALTZ
Editorial Director

WE REALLY ARE SWEET . . .

"I love whenever someone grabs communal forks for everyone before we all dig into one pan. There's a strong sense of community and also low-key disgust that we dig into one massive pot until it's completely gone."
—JULIA SMITH, Senior Editor of Content & Video Strategy

"This is not a joke, but one of my fondest memories this past year was telling my edit corner coworkers I'd officially gained the Delish 15 (the inaugural weight you always gain working at this place). We were sitting in Pizza Lounge talking about who knows what when I brought it up, and my announcement was followed by an 'AWWWWW!' and hugs all around. It made me tear up in a happy way, not because I'd gained fifteen pounds, but like I truly belonged."
—TESS KOMAN, Features Editor

"This one's from my birthday last year. I'm notorious for eating giant carrots in the kitchen as snacks, so the girls made me a giant carrot cake. With an amazing pun on it, no less! I think it's safe to say we do birthdays bigger than most places."
—LENA ABRAHAM, Food Editor

"I almost cried when the kitchen team made me this Deb (my dog) cake for my birthday. It was the most thoughtful and most delicious (peanut butter on peanut butter on peanut butter) birthday cake EVER, and I want it every year from now on."
—LAUREN MIYASHIRO, Food Director

"This picture is the 1st place sweetest moment. I felt so much love—I bet no one has seen me smile this big. Makinze doesn't know yet, but we're now engaged and will be playing Rupert Holmes's 'Escape (The Piña Colada Song)' at our wedding."
—JUNE XIE, Kitchen Assistant

CHAPTER ONE

COOKIE MONSTERS

FLOURLESS FUDGE
COOKIES, PG 45!

DEATH BY CHOCOLATE COOKIES

TOTAL TIME: 1 HR / MAKES 36

Only true chocoholics (read: everyone at Delish) will be able to handle this triple threat: cocoa powder, chocolate chips, and melty ganache. Don't even think about skipping the flaky sea salt—it actually helps these cookies taste a little sweeter.

2 cups all-purpose flour

¾ cup unsweetened cocoa powder

1 teaspoon baking soda

½ teaspoon kosher salt

1 cup (2 sticks) butter, softened

⅔ cup granulated sugar

⅔ cup packed brown sugar

2 large eggs

1 teaspoon pure vanilla extract

1 cup semisweet choco-late chips

1 cup dark chocolate chips

Ganache

Flaky sea salt

1. Preheat oven to 350°F and line two large baking sheets with parchment paper.

2. In a medium bowl, whisk together flour, cocoa powder, baking soda, and kosher salt.

3. In a large bowl using a hand mixer, beat together butter and sugars until light and fluffy. Add eggs, one at a time, and beat until incorporated, then add vanilla. Add dry ingredients to wet ingredients and beat until combined, then fold in semisweet and dark chocolate chips.

4. Using a medium cookie scoop, scoop balls of dough (about 1½ tablespoons each) onto prepared baking sheets, spacing cookies 2 inches apart.

5. Bake until centers are set, 9 to 12 minutes. Let cookies cool on pans 5 minutes, then transfer to wire racks to cool completely. Repeat with remaining dough.

6. Dip cookies halfway in ganache and return to baking sheets. Sprinkle dipped sides with flaky salt. Let set before serving.

▶ GANACHE

Put ¾ cup **DARK CHOCOLATE CHIPS** in a large heatproof bowl. In a small saucepan over medium heat, heat ½ cup **HEAVY CREAM** until steaming and bubbles form around the edge. Pour over chocolate and let sit 5 minutes, then whisk until chocolate has completely melted and mixture is combined.

CHOCOLATE CHIP COOKIE DIPPERS

TOTAL TIME: 40 MIN / MAKES 24

When Lauren, our resident cookie monster, wanted to make these "dunkers," we all freaked out—who doesn't love dipping a cookie in milk?! You'll wish every cookie came in this brilliant stick shape.

¾ cup (1½ sticks) butter, softened

1 cup packed brown sugar

¼ cup plus 2 tablespoons granulated sugar

2 large eggs

1 teaspoon pure vanilla extract

2¼ cups all-purpose flour

¾ teaspoon baking soda

¾ teaspoon kosher salt

1¾ cups mini chocolate chips, divided

1. Preheat oven to 350°F and line a large baking sheet with parchment paper, leaving a 1-inch overhang on each side of pan.

2. In a large bowl using a hand mixer, beat butter and sugars until light and fluffy. Add eggs and vanilla and beat until combined. Add flour, baking soda, and salt and mix until just incorporated. Fold in ¾ cup of chocolate chips.

3. Press dough into prepared pan in an even layer and sprinkle with remaining ½ cup chocolate chips, gently pressing them into dough.

4. Bake until edges are golden, about 20 minutes. Let cool in pan 10 minutes, then transfer to a wire rack to cool completely.

5. Using a pizza cutter or sharp knife, slice cookie crosswise into long strips, then halve them to make shorter sticks.

INSIDE-OUT RED VELVET COOKIES

TOTAL TIME: 1 HR 10 MIN / MAKES 18

We all know the best part of a slice of red velvet cake is the cream cheese frosting—imagine a whole crackly cookie stuffed with it.

FOR THE FILLING

1 (8-ounce) block cream cheese, softened

½ cup powdered sugar

Pinch kosher salt

FOR THE COOKIES

½ cup (1 stick) butter, softened

½ cup granulated sugar

¼ cup packed brown sugar

1 large egg

1 tablespoon red food coloring

1 teaspoon pure vanilla extract

1¼ cups all-purpose flour

¼ cup unsweetened cocoa powder

½ teaspoon baking powder

¼ teaspoon kosher salt

1. Preheat oven to 350°F and line two large baking sheets with parchment paper.

2. Make filling: In a small bowl, whisk together cream cheese, powdered sugar, and salt until smooth. Cover with plastic wrap and freeze until slightly firm, about 30 minutes.

3. Make cookie dough: In a large bowl using a hand mixer, beat butter and sugars until light and fluffy. Beat in egg, food coloring, and vanilla until incorporated. Add flour, cocoa powder, baking powder, and salt and mix until just combined.

4. Make cookies: Using a medium cookie scoop, scoop balls of dough (about 1½ tablespoons each) and flatten each into a pancake-like circle. Top with about 2 teaspoons cream cheese filling and cover with dough, pinching edges to seal and adding more dough if necessary to completely enclose. Transfer to prepared baking sheets, spacing cookies 3 inches apart. Repeat with remaining ingredients.

5. Bake until cookies are set and crackly on top, 15 to 17 minutes.

ULTIMATE SNICKERDOODLES

TOTAL TIME: 1 HR / MAKES 13

We're not lying when we say these are kind of a big deal. (We were honestly surprised to see what a cult following they have in our audience.) Our version is bigger, which means better, obvs, and rolled in that cinnamon-sugar goodness TWICE.

2½ cups all-purpose flour

1 tablespoon plus 1 teaspoon ground cinnamon, divided

2 teaspoons cream of tartar

1 teaspoon baking soda

1 teaspoon kosher salt

1 cup (2 sticks) butter, softened

1¼ cups granulated sugar, divided

½ cup packed brown sugar

2 large eggs

1. Preheat oven to 350°F and line two large baking sheets with parchment paper.

2. In a medium bowl, whisk together flour, 1 teaspoon of cinnamon, cream of tartar, baking soda, and salt.

3. In a large bowl using a hand mixer, beat butter, 1 cup of granulated sugar, and brown sugar until light and fluffy. Add eggs, one at a time, and beat until combined. Add dry ingredients to wet ingredients and beat until combined.

4. In a shallow bowl, whisk together remaining ¼ cup granulated sugar and 1 tablespoon cinnamon.

5. Using a large cookie scoop, scoop mounds of dough (about 3 tablespoons each) and roll into a ball, then roll in cinnamon-sugar and transfer to prepared baking sheets, spacing cookies 2 inches apart. Bake until cookies begin to crack, about 13 minutes.

BEST-EVER CHOCOLATE CHIP COOKIES

TOTAL TIME: 50 MIN / MAKES 15

Chocolate chip cookies are VERY personal: Everyone has an opinion on what makes the best one—including us. Ours is soft, with the perfect amount of chew (thanks to the extra egg yolk!), and never cakey. We're flaky-salt fiends, so finishing these with a sprinkle is mandatory.

1 cup (2 sticks) butter

1 cup packed brown sugar

½ cup granulated sugar

1 large egg

1 large egg yolk

1 teaspoon pure vanilla extract

2 cups all-purpose flour

1 teaspoon baking soda

1 teaspoon kosher salt

¼ teaspoon ground cinnamon

1½ cups semisweet chocolate chips

3 ounces chocolate, chopped (about ⅓ cup)

Flaky sea salt, for garnish

1. Preheat oven to 325°F and line two large baking sheets with parchment paper.

2. In a small saucepan over medium heat, melt butter. Bring it to a boil and cook 1 minute.

3. Place sugars in a large bowl, then pour hot butter over sugars. Beat with a hand mixer until combined. Add egg, egg yolk, and vanilla and beat until light and creamy, 2 minutes.

4. In another large bowl, whisk together flour, baking soda, kosher salt, and cinnamon. Add dry ingredients to wet ingredients and beat until just combined with just a few white streaks remaining. Fold in chocolate chips and chopped chocolate.

5. Using a large cookie scoop, scoop balls of dough (about 3 tablespoons each) onto prepared baking sheets, spacing cookies 3 inches apart. Sprinkle with flaky salt.

6. Bake until edges are golden and almost set in the middle, 14 to 15 minutes (cookies will still look slightly underdone).

PEANUT BUTTER BLOSSOMS

TOTAL TIME: 20 MIN / MAKES 30

Our food director Lauren made these every Christmas Eve when she was growing up, so she demanded that Delish have its own version. The cookies are typically made with shortening for a softer texture, but our recipe is flawless with butter. Skip natural peanut butter here; use the super-creamy kind you grew up with.

1¾ cups all-purpose flour

1 teaspoon baking soda

½ teaspoon kosher salt

½ cup (1 stick) butter, softened

½ cup smooth peanut butter

½ cup packed brown sugar

¼ cup granulated sugar, plus more for rolling

1 large egg

2 tablespoons milk

1 teaspoon pure vanilla extract

30 Hershey's Kisses (from a 12-ounce bag)

1. Preheat oven to 375°F and line two large baking sheets with parchment paper.

2. In a medium bowl, whisk together flour, baking soda, and salt.

3. In a large bowl using a hand mixer, beat butter and peanut butter until smooth. Add sugars and beat until light and fluffy. Beat in egg, then add milk and vanilla. Gradually add dry ingredients to wet ingredients, beating on low until just combined.

4. Using a small cookie scoop, scoop a tablespoon-size ball of dough. Roll into a ball, then roll in granulated sugar to coat. Transfer to prepared baking sheet and repeat with remaining dough, spacing cookies 2 inches apart.

5. Bake until cookies have poofed and no longer look raw, 8 to 10 minutes. (They won't brown!)

6. Immediately top each with a Hershey's Kiss, then let cool on pans slightly. Repeat with remaining dough.

BIRTHDAY CAKE COOKIES

TOTAL TIME: 30 MIN / MAKES 22

We know plenty of people who would way rather down a dozen of these rainbow cookies than a slice of birthday cake. Plus, they use the most brilliant shortcut—cake mix!—which means they only require six ingredients.

---

1 (15.25-ounce) box Funfetti cake mix

1 teaspoon baking powder

2 large eggs

½ cup (1 stick) butter, softened

1 teaspoon pure vanilla extract

½ cup rainbow sprinkles

1. Preheat oven to 350°F and line two large baking sheets with parchment paper.

2. In a large bowl, whisk together cake mix and baking powder. Add eggs, butter, and vanilla and, using a hand mixer, beat until well combined. Mix in sprinkles.

3. Using a medium cookie scoop, scoop balls of dough (about 1½ tablespoons each) onto prepared baking sheets, spacing cookies 1 inch apart.

4. Bake until lightly golden, 12 to 13 minutes.

You can **SPIKE THE MILK** with bourbon, vodka, chocolate liqueur, even RumChata.

MILK & COOKIE SHOTS

TOTAL TIME: 35 MIN / MAKES 12

The type of shot we take when we're really trying to party.
This muffin tin hack turns store-bought cookie dough into the
most fun (and edible!) vessel for throwing back booze. During the
holidays, get the whole family tipsy by swapping the milk for eggnog.

Cooking spray

1 (32-ounce) log
refrigerated chocolate
chip cookie dough

1 cup semisweet
chocolate chips

2 tablespoons coconut
oil (or butter)

Ice

Baileys Irish Cream, for
serving

Milk, for serving

1. Preheat oven to 350°F and grease a muffin tin with cooking spray.

2. Fill each cup with a small ball of cookie dough, pressing down to form a well. Bake until cookies are lightly golden, 10 to 12 minutes.

3. Grease bottom of a small shot glass with cooking spray and, while cookies are still warm, press into center of each cookie to form a cup. Let cool in pans 15 minutes, then transfer to wire racks to cool completely.

4. In a heatproof bowl, microwave chocolate chips and coconut oil in 30-second intervals until melted.

5. Using a knife, remove cookie cups from pan and transfer to a baking sheet or platter. Line each cookie cup with melted chocolate and refrigerate until set, about 15 minutes.

6. In a cocktail shaker filled with ice, combine equal parts Baileys and milk. Shake, then pour into each cookie shot glass. Serve immediately.

PEANUT BUTTER STUFFED COOKIES

TOTAL TIME: 35 MIN / MAKES 22

These cookies pay homage to one of our all-time favorite ingredients. Peanut butter stuffed inside a killer peanut butter cookie is proof that too much is never enough. The weirdest part: The PB center stays gooey even after the cookies have cooled.

FOR THE FILLING

1 cup creamy peanut butter

½ cup powdered sugar

FOR THE COOKIES

½ cup (1 stick) butter, softened

½ cup creamy peanut butter

½ cup packed brown sugar

¼ cup granulated sugar, plus more for rolling

1 large egg

1 teaspoon pure vanilla extract

1½ cups all-purpose flour

½ teaspoon baking soda

½ teaspoon kosher salt

1. Preheat oven to 375°F and line two large baking sheets with parchment paper.

2. Make filling: In a medium bowl, stir together peanut butter and powdered sugar until smooth. Using a small cookie scoop, scoop 22 balls of peanut butter mixture onto one prepared baking sheet and freeze until firm, 30 minutes.

3. Make cookies: In a large bowl using a hand mixer, beat butter, peanut butter, and sugars until fluffy. Add egg and vanilla and beat until incorporated, then add flour, baking soda, and salt and beat until just combined.

4. Using a medium cookie scoop, scoop 22 balls of dough (about 1½ tablespoons each) and flatten each into a pancake-like circle. Top with a frozen peanut butter ball and cover with dough, pinching edges to seal and adding more dough if necessary to completely enclose. Transfer to prepared baking sheets and repeat with remaining dough and frozen peanut butter, spacing cookies 2 inches apart.

5. Bake until golden on the bottom, 12 to 15 minutes.

CHERRY CHIP COOKIES

TOTAL TIME: 40 MIN / MAKES 24

Life hack: Never turn down a baking project with maraschino cherries. Those electric-red gems are like happiness in a jar. These make amazing cookie ice cream sandwiches—add a couple of scoops of vanilla and they'll taste like a sundae.

2¼ cups all-purpose flour

1 teaspoon baking soda

¾ teaspoon kosher salt

1 cup (2 sticks) butter, softened

¾ cup packed brown sugar

½ cup granulated sugar

2 large eggs

1 teaspoon pure vanilla extract

2 cups semisweet chocolate chips

¾ cup chopped maraschino cherries

1. Preheat oven to 350°F and line two baking sheets with parchment paper.

2. In a medium bowl, whisk together flour, baking soda, and salt.

3. In a large bowl using a hand mixer, beat butter and sugars until light and fluffy. Add eggs, one at a time, and beat until incorporated, then add vanilla. Add dry ingredients to wet ingredients and beat until just combined, then fold in chocolate chips and cherries.

4. Using a large cookie scoop, scoop balls of dough (about 3 tablespoons each) onto prepared baking sheets, spacing cookies 2 inches apart.

5. Bake until set, 12 to 15 minutes.

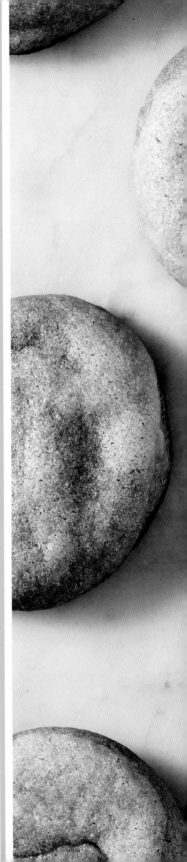

EARTH DAY COOKIES

TOTAL TIME: 30 MIN / MAKES 18

The technique for creating these two-toned cookies is so easy, even a kid could pull it off. (Trust us, we've made these with many a child.) If you'd rather make the sugar cookie dough from scratch, see our recipe on page 198.

1 (17.5-ounce) bag sugar cookie mix, plus ingredients called for on package

6 drops blue food coloring

6 drops green food coloring

1. Preheat oven to 375°F and line two large baking sheets with parchment paper.

2. Prepare sugar cookie dough according to package instructions. Divide dough between two bowls. Color one bowl with blue food coloring and the other with green food coloring.

3. Pull out pieces of each color and shape into tablespoon-sized balls, patching if necessary to create an Earth effect. Transfer dough balls to prepared baking sheets, spacing cookies 1 inch apart.

4. Bake until edges are firm, 8 to 9 minutes (try to prevent any browning).

31 AMAZING MIX-INS FOR CHOCOLATE CHIP COOKIE DOUGH

Mix in some of these extras to make the classic even more addictive.

1
REESE'S MINIS PEANUT BUTTER CUPS

2
CORNFLAKES

3
MINI MARSH-MALLOWS

4
CRYSTALLIZED GINGER

5
CHOPPED PRETZELS

6
ORANGE ZEST

7
CARAMEL CORN

8
CAYENNE PEPPER

9
FREEZE-DRIED STRAW-BERRIES

10
SOFT CARAMELS

11
RICE KRISPIES

12
MALTED MILK BALLS

13
LUCKY CHARMS

14
CHOPPED COOKED BACON

15
TOASTED COCONUT

16
DRIED CHERRIES

17
NUTELLA

18
BUTTER-SCOTCH CHIPS

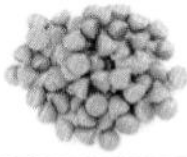

19
CRUSHED GRAHAM CRACKERS

20
CHOPPED BUTTER-FINGERS

21
TOFFEE BITS

22
CANDY CANES

23
GRANOLA

24
RUFFLES

25
CANDIED NUTS

26
MINI OREOS

27
TAHINI

28
CHOCOLATE-COVERED ESPRESSO BEANS

29
REESE'S PIECES

30
POPPY SEEDS

31
COOKIE BUTTER

PUMPKIN CHOCOLATE CHIP COOKIES

TOTAL TIME: 1 HR 30 MIN / MAKES 35

Saying these cookies "went viral" is an understatement—everyone you know made these at one point or another. It's not a crisp cookie—the canned pumpkin gives them a soft texture— but that's the magic.

2¼ cups all-purpose flour

1 teaspoon baking soda

1 teaspoon pumpkin pie spice

½ teaspoon kosher salt

1 cup (2 sticks) butter, softened

¾ cup packed brown sugar

½ cup granulated sugar

¾ cup pumpkin puree

1 large egg

2 teaspoons pure vanilla extract

2 cups semisweet chocolate chips

1. Preheat oven to 375°F and line two large baking sheets with parchment paper.

2. In a medium bowl, whisk together flour, baking soda, pumpkin pie spice, and salt.

3. In a large bowl using a hand mixer, beat butter and sugars until light and fluffy. Add pumpkin, egg, and vanilla and beat until incorporated. Add dry ingredients to wet ingredients and beat until just combined, then fold in chocolate chips.

4. Refrigerate dough 30 minutes.

5. Using a medium cookie scoop, scoop balls of dough (about 1½ tablespoons each) onto prepared baking sheets, spacing cookies 2 inches apart.

6. Bake until puffed up and golden around edges, about 12 minutes. Repeat with remaining dough.

CARROT CAKE COOKIES

TOTAL TIME: 1 HR 15 MIN / MAKES 36

Carrot cake happens to be one of our all-time favorite desserts at Delish, so turning it into a cookie was a no-brainer. These have a whole cup of grated carrots and 2 cups of oats inside, soooo that cancels out the rest of the calories, right?

1½ cups all-purpose flour

1 teaspoon baking soda

1 teaspoon ground cinnamon

¼ teaspoon ground nutmeg

½ teaspoon kosher salt

¾ cup (1½ sticks) butter, softened

1 cup packed brown sugar

½ cup granulated sugar

2 large eggs

1 teaspoon pure vanilla extract

2 cups old-fashioned rolled oats

1 cup packed shredded carrots (about 2 medium)

¾ cup unsweetened shredded coconut

½ cup raisins

Vanilla Glaze

1. Make cookies: Preheat oven to 350°F and line two large baking sheets with parchment paper.

2. In a medium bowl, whisk together flour, baking soda, cinnamon, nutmeg, and salt.

3. In a large bowl using a hand mixer, beat butter and sugars until light and fluffy. Add eggs, one at a time, and beat until incorporated, then add vanilla. Add dry ingredients to wet ingredients and beat until fully combined, then mix in oats, carrots, coconut, and raisins until just combined.

4. Using a medium cookie scoop, scoop balls of dough (about 1½ tablespoons each) onto prepared baking sheets, spacing cookies 1 inch apart.

5. Bake until golden, 16 to 18 minutes. Let cool on pans 10 minutes, then transfer to wire racks to cool completely. Repeat with remaining dough.

6. Drizzle Vanilla Glaze over cookies and let harden before serving.

VANILLA GLAZE

In a medium bowl, beat together
1 cup **POWDERED SUGAR**, 1 ounce
softened **CREAM CHEESE**,
4 teaspoons **MILK**, and ¼ teaspoon
pure **VANILLA EXTRACT.**

BANANA PUDDING COOKIES

TOTAL TIME: 45 MIN / MAKES 28

Our love for banana pudding runs deep. We've never made a twist on the Southern dessert we didn't like—cheesecake, fudge, boozy shots. If you wish you could eat banana bread in cookie form, these are for you.

¾ cup (1½ sticks) butter, softened

½ cup granulated sugar

¼ cup packed brown sugar

2 bananas

1 large egg

1 teaspoon pure vanilla extract

1 (3.5-ounce) packet instant vanilla pudding

2 cups all-purpose flour

1 teaspoon baking soda

½ teaspoon kosher salt

½ cup crushed Nilla wafers (about 13), plus more for garnish

Cool Whip, for serving

1. Preheat oven to 350°F and line two large baking sheets with parchment paper.

2. In a large bowl using a hand mixer, beat butter and sugars until light and fluffy.

3. In a small bowl, mash 1½ bananas (reserve remaining ½ banana for garnish). Add mashed bananas, egg, vanilla, and pudding mix to butter mixture and beat until combined.

4. Add flour, baking soda, and salt and mix until just combined, then fold in Nilla wafers.

5. Using a medium cookie scoop, scoop balls of dough (about 1½ tablespoons each) onto prepared baking sheets, spacing cookies 1 inch apart.

6. Bake until golden, 12 to 14 minutes. Let cool on pans 10 minutes, then transfer to wire racks to cool completely.

7. When ready to serve, thinly slice remaining ½ banana. Top each cookie with a dollop of Cool Whip, more crushed Nilla wafers, and a banana slice.

 If you're making these in **ADVANCE**, don't top them until you're ready to serve.

PUMPKIN WHOOPIE PIES

TOTAL TIME: 1 HR 15 MIN / MAKES 16

Is a whoopie pie a cookie or a mini cake? Not really sure we care—we only know that we start baking these as soon as pumpkin spice season hits. The cream cheese filling is killer.

3 cups all-purpose flour

1 tablespoon pumpkin pie spice

1 teaspoon baking powder

1 teaspoon baking soda

1 teaspoon kosher salt

2 cups packed brown sugar

½ cup vegetable oil

½ cup (1 stick) butter, softened

2 large eggs

1 (15-ounce) can pumpkin puree, preferably chilled

1 teaspoon pure vanilla extract

FOR THE FILLING

1 (8-ounce) block cream cheese, softened

½ cup (1 stick) butter, softened

3 cups powdered sugar

2 tablespoons maple syrup

1. Preheat oven to 350°F and line two large baking sheets with parchment paper.

2. In a medium bowl, whisk together flour, pumpkin pie spice, baking powder, baking soda, and salt.

3. In a large bowl using a hand mixer, beat brown sugar, oil, butter, eggs, pumpkin puree, and vanilla until smooth. Add dry ingredients to wet ingredients and beat until combined. (The dough will be sticky and soft.)

4. Using a medium cookie scoop, scoop mounds of dough (about 1½ tablespoons each) onto prepared baking sheets, spacing cookies at least 2 inches apart.

5. Bake until springy to the touch, 12 to 15 minutes. Transfer cookies to wire racks to cool completely.

6. Make filling: In a large bowl using a hand mixer, beat cream cheese and remaining butter until fluffy. Add powdered sugar, maple syrup, and vanilla and beat until light and fluffy.

7. Spread filling onto bottoms of half the cookies. Top with remaining cookies, bottom-side down.

8. Serve immediately or store in an airtight container in fridge up to 3 days.

If maple syrup isn't your thing, replace it with two teaspoons of pure **VANILLA EXTRACT** in the filling.

FLOURLESS FUDGE COOKIES

TOTAL TIME: 30 MIN / MAKES 30

Every few months, Jo goes through a "gluten-free" phase. And it lasts for like, 20 minutes. These intensely chewy, rich cookies are just the thing if you're avoiding gluten—they feel completely decadent and not the least bit like you're missing out.

Cooking spray

2½ cups powdered sugar

¾ cup unsweetened cocoa powder

¼ teaspoon kosher salt

4 large egg whites

½ teaspoon pure vanilla extract

1½ cups semisweet chocolate chips

1. Preheat oven to 350°F and line two large baking sheets with parchment paper and lightly grease with cooking spray.

2. In a large bowl, whisk together powdered sugar, cocoa powder, and salt. Add egg whites and vanilla and whisk until combined, then fold in chocolate chips.

3. Using a medium cookie scoop, scoop about 1½ tablespoons batter onto prepared baking sheets, spacing cookies 2 inches apart.

4. Bake until set, 10 to 12 minutes. Let cookies cool completely on parchment before trying to remove. Repeat with remaining batter.

5 AMAZING THINGS TO DO WITH SUGAR COOKIE DOUGH

A log of store-bought stuff can become so much more.

1
SUGAR COOKIE POPS

Place 1 cup **rainbow sprinkles** in a shallow bowl. Using a small cookie scoop, scoop tablespoon-size balls from 1 (16.5-ounce) log **sugar cookie dough** and roll in sprinkles. Insert wooden ice pop sticks into dough balls and transfer to two parchment-lined baking sheets. Bake at 350°F until lightly golden, 12 to 15 minutes. Let cool before serving. (pictured left)

2
RAINBOW COOKIE PIZZA

On a lightly floured sheet of parchment paper, roll out 1 (16.5-ounce) log **sugar cookie dough** into a 10-inch circle. Transfer to a baking sheet and bake at 350°F until edges are lightly golden, 20 minutes. Beat 1 (8-ounce) block **cream cheese** and 4 tablespoons (½ stick) softened **butter** until smooth. Add 1½ cups **powdered sugar**, 1 teaspoon **pure vanilla extract**, and a pinch of **kosher salt** and beat until smooth. Spread frosting onto cooled cookie and top with **blueberries** and sliced **strawberries**, **mango**, **banana**, and **kiwi**.

3
SUGAR COOKIE MUFFINS

In a large bowl, break up 1 (16.5-ounce) log **sugar cookie dough** (at room temperature). Add 1 large **egg**, ½ cup mashed **banana**, 2 teaspoons **lemon juice**, and ½ teaspoon **baking powder**. Beat until smooth, then fold in 1½ cups **blueberries**. Transfer batter to a greased muffin tin and bake at 350°F until edges are golden and a toothpick inserted into the center of each comes out clean, about 18 minutes.

4
NUTELLA SANDWICH COOKIES

Slice 1 (16.5-ounce) log **sugar cookie dough** into ¼-inch-thick rounds. Space 2 inches apart on two parchment-lined baking sheets and sprinkle with **cinnamon-sugar**. Bake at 350°F until edges are lightly golden, about 10 minutes. Repeat with remaining dough. Let cool completely, then flip over half the cookies and dollop each with 1 tablespoon **Nutella**. Sandwich with remaining cookies.

5
SNICKERS-STUFFED COOKIES

Slice 1 (16.5-ounce) log **sugar cookie dough** into twelve ½-inch-thick rounds. Flatten each between your hands and top with a fun-size **Snickers**. Cover with dough, pinching to seal. Transfer to two parchment-lined baking sheets, spacing cookies 4 inches apart. Bake at 350°F until edges are golden, about 13 minutes. Let cool slightly, then drizzle with **caramel**.

A **KITCHEN TORCH** is good for:
- melting cheese
- caramelizing sugar
- toasting marshmallows

CRÈME BRÛLÉE COOKIES

TOTAL TIME: 50 MIN / MAKES 40

Caramelized sugar > frosting. These melted our brains when we first tasted them. To get the mandatory burnt crackly top, you kind of do need a kitchen torch. (We've attempted to achieve the classic textural greatness under the broiler, and it's just not the same.)

FOR THE COOKIES

¾ cup (1½ sticks) butter, softened

½ cup packed brown sugar

½ cup granulated sugar

1 large egg

1 tablespoon pure vanilla extract

2 cups all-purpose flour

2 teaspoons cornstarch

1 teaspoon baking soda

¼ teaspoon kosher salt

FOR THE FROSTING

1 (8-ounce) block cream cheese, softened

1¼ cups powdered sugar

1 teaspoon pure vanilla extract

¼ cup granulated sugar

1. Make cookies: Preheat oven to 350°F and line two large baking sheets with parchment paper.

2. In a large bowl using a hand mixer, beat butter and sugars until light and fluffy. Add egg and vanilla and beat until incorporated.

3. In a medium bowl, whisk together flour, cornstarch, baking soda, and salt. Add dry ingredients and beat until combined.

4. Using a small cookie scoop, scoop tablespoon-size balls of dough onto prepared baking sheets, spacing cookies 1 inch apart. Press down lightly on each cookie to flatten.

5. Bake until edges are just starting to brown, 7 to 8 minutes. Let cookies cool completely.

6. Make frosting: In a large bowl using a hand mixer, beat cream cheese until smooth. Add powdered sugar and vanilla and mix until combined.

7. Place granulated sugar in a shallow bowl. Spread frosting onto tops of cookies, then press into sugar to coat.

8. Using a kitchen torch, caramelize sugar on top. Let cool before serving.

chip happens.

BUCKEYE COOKIES

TOTAL TIME: 1 HR 20 MIN / MAKES 22

Why, yes, this is one of *three* desserts in this book stuffed with peanut butter—but who's counting?! Our love for buckeyes—chocolate-dipped peanut butter–fudge candies—knows no limits.

FOR THE FILLING

1¼ cups creamy peanut butter

⅓ cup powdered sugar

FOR THE COOKIES

¾ cup (1½ sticks) butter, softened

¾ cup packed brown sugar

½ cup granulated sugar, plus more for rolling

1 large egg

1 teaspoon pure vanilla extract

1¼ cups all-purpose flour

¾ cup unsweetened cocoa powder

¾ teaspoon baking soda

¾ teaspoon kosher salt

1. Preheat oven to 350°F and line two large baking sheets with parchment paper.

2. Make filling: In a medium bowl, stir together peanut butter and powdered sugar until smooth. Using a small cookie scoop, scoop mixture into 22 balls onto prepared baking sheet and freeze until firm, 30 minutes.

3. Make cookies: In a large bowl using a hand mixer, beat butter and sugars until light and fluffy, then add egg and vanilla and beat until incorporated. Add flour, cocoa powder, baking soda, and salt and beat until combined.

4. Scoop a heaping tablespoon of dough and flatten into a pancake-like circle. Top with a frozen peanut butter ball, then wrap edges of dough around peanut butter ball and pinch to seal, adding more dough if necessary to completely enclose peanut butter. Roll stuffed cookie dough ball in sugar and transfer to prepared baking sheets, spacing cookies 2 inches apart. Repeat with remaining dough.

5. Bake until cookies are set, about 12 minutes.

TROPICAL TOPPING

- 1 cup Cool Whip
- Toasted sweetened coconut flakes
- 24 pineapple wedges
- 24 maraschino cherries

PIÑA COLADA COOKIE CUPS

TOTAL TIME: 1 HR 30 MIN / MAKES 24

Warning: This super-addicting filling tastes like a cross between a slice of cheesecake and a piña colada. Partying with kids? These still make a cute dessert—just skip the booze!

FOR THE COOKIE CUPS
Cooking spray

1 cup (2 sticks) butter, softened

1 cup packed brown sugar

½ cup granulated sugar

2 large eggs

1 teaspoon pure vanilla extract

2½ cups all-purpose flour

1 teaspoon baking powder

½ teaspoon ground cinnamon

½ teaspoon kosher salt

FOR THE FILLING
1 (8-ounce) block cream cheese, softened

2 cups powdered sugar

1 tablespoon pineapple juice

1 tablespoon white rum

1. Make cookie cups: Preheat oven to 350°F and grease two muffin tins with cooking spray.

2. In a large bowl using a hand mixer, beat butter and sugars until fluffy. Add eggs and vanilla and beat until incorporated. Add flour, baking powder, cinnamon, and salt and mix until just combined.

3. Using a medium cookie scoop, scoop balls of dough (about 1½ tablespoons each) into prepared muffin tin cups and press with your fingers to flatten. Bake until cookie cups are golden and set, 15 to 20 minutes.

4. Grease the bottom of a small shot glass with cooking spray and press down into center of each cookie to form a cup. Let cool in pan 15 minutes, then transfer to wire racks to cool completely.

5. Meanwhile, make filling: In a large bowl using a hand mixer, beat cream cheese, powdered sugar, pineapple juice, and rum until smooth.

6. Spoon filling into cookie cups. Dollop each with Cool Whip, then top with toasted coconut, a pineapple wedge, and a cherry.

MACARON PARLOUR

NEW YORK

THE NOW infamous Cheetos Macaron began as a trick on a classic treat, originally meant for Macaron Parlour's wife-and-husband founders, Christina Ha and Simon Tung, to hand out to unsuspecting trick-or-treaters for Halloween. But this was Halloween 2012, when Hurricane Sandy hit. The bakery's entire block lost power, people were costume-clad while vacating their apartments, and almost no one was coming into the store, which was . . . unfortunate, since Christina and Simon had made hundreds of black Cheetos-flavored macarons to hand out.

Still, the fifteen or so trick-or-treaters who did make it to the bakery that evening were enough to make the macaron go viral. The flavor became so popular, fans would freak every time the Parlour dropped it from their rotating lineup, prompting Christina and Simon to make an orange version that's always available.

Ironically, the offbeat dessert recipe—inspired by a bag of Cheetos-colored cheese powder—didn't take many tries to perfect. "It's one of the few recipes we nailed on the first try. It rarely happens that way," Christina says. "It's a testament to my love for Cheetos." But actually getting customers to eat the macarons—which start savory and have a sweet white chocolate finish—rather than just 'gram them was hard. "A lot of people come and look at it and laugh, and they're like, 'Eh, no, I'm gonna get the lemon,'" Christina says. "As a business, you want to be taken seriously, but we might as well have fun while doing it."

MACARON PARLOUR'S
CHEETOS MACARONS

TOTAL TIME: 2 HR 30 MIN / MAKES 15

1 cup heavy cream

1 (2-ounce) bag Cheetos Puffs

1 cup chopped white chocolate, melted

¼ teaspoon kosher salt

1½ cups powdered sugar

1¾ cups almond flour

4 large egg whites

¾ cup granulated sugar

Red and orange gel food coloring

Powdered cheese dust

1. Make ganache: In a small saucepan over medium heat, bring heavy cream to a boil with Cheetos. Turn off heat and let mixture sit for at least 1 hour. Strain Cheetos out of heavy cream.

2. In a medium bowl, stir together melted white chocolate, Cheetos-infused heavy cream, and salt. Refrigerate 2 hours.

3. Make macarons: Preheat oven to 325°F and line two large baking sheets with parchment paper.

4. In a large bowl, sift together powdered sugar and almond flour. In the bowl of a stand mixer fitted with a whisk attachment, whip egg whites and sugar until stiff peaks form. Gradually fold meringue and food coloring into dry ingredients until just combined.

5. Transfer batter to a piping bag fitted with a round tip. Pipe 1¾-inch rounds onto prepared baking sheets.

6. Bake 12 minutes. Let cool completely. Repeat with remaining batter.

7. Lay half the macaron shells down with their flat bottoms facing up. Pipe Cheetos ganache onto macaron shells, then sandwich with remaining macaron shells and sprinkle with cheese dust.

8. Refrigerate macarons 24 hours before serving.

STRAWBERRY SHORTCAKE COOKIES

TOTAL TIME: 45 MIN / MAKES 12

Covering the cream cheese with cookie dough can be a messy task (especially with the fresh strawberries!), but power through. We promise it's worth it.

Cooking spray

¾ cup chopped strawberries

1 tablespoon lemon juice

½ cup plus 1 tablespoon granulated sugar, divided

2 cups all-purpose flour

½ teaspoon baking powder

¼ teaspoon kosher salt

½ cup (1 stick) butter, softened

¼ cup packed brown sugar

1 large egg

1 teaspoon pure vanilla extract

FOR THE FILLING

¼ cup cream cheese, softened

3 tablespoons powdered sugar

Zest of 1 lemon

Coarse sugar, for garnish

1. Preheat oven to 350°F and line two large baking sheets with parchment paper and grease with cooking spray.

2. In a small bowl, stir together strawberries, lemon juice, and 1 tablespoon granulated sugar until combined. Let sit 10 minutes, then drain.

3. In a medium bowl, whisk together flour, baking powder, and salt.

4. In a large bowl using a hand mixer, beat butter, remaining ½ cup granulated sugar, and brown sugar until light and fluffy. Beat in egg and vanilla. Add dry ingredients to wet ingredients and beat until just combined. Gently fold in strawberries.

5. Make filling: In a medium bowl using a hand mixer, beat cream cheese, powdered sugar, and lemon zest until smooth.

6. Using a medium cookie scoop, scoop 24 balls of dough (about 1½ tablespoons each) and flatten each into a pancake-like circle. Top half the dough pieces with 1½ teaspoons cream cheese filling each, then cover with remaining dough and pinch to seal. Roll gently into balls and transfer to prepared baking sheets, spacing cookies 2 inches apart.

7. Sprinkle cookies with coarse sugar and bake until set and just golden around edges, about 18 minutes.

Don't **CHILL THE DOUGH** for longer than an hour, or your marshmallows won't melt!

S'MORES STUFFED COOKIES

TOTAL TIME: 30 MIN / MAKES 8

When our food editor Lena pitched this insanity, we didn't believe she could do it. A whole s'more—graham and all—wrapped INSIDE a chocolate chip cookie? GTFO. But the result is just as melty and gooey as you'd imagine.

FOR THE COOKIES

2¾ cups all-purpose flour

1 teaspoon baking soda

¾ teaspoon kosher salt

1½ cups (2½ sticks) butter, softened

1 cup packed brown sugar

½ cup granulated sugar

2 large eggs

2 teaspoons pure vanilla extract

2 cups semisweet chocolate chips

FOR THE S'MORES

16 graham cracker squares

4 marshmallows, halved lengthwise

8 chocolate squares

1. Preheat oven to 375°F and line two large baking sheets with parchment paper.

2. Make cookies: In a medium bowl, whisk together flour, baking soda, and salt.

3. In a large bowl using a hand mixer, beat butter and sugars until light and fluffy. Add eggs, one at a time, and beat until incorporated, then add vanilla. Add dry ingredients to wet ingredients and beat until just combined, then fold in chocolate chips.

4. Make s'mores: Between two graham cracker squares, sandwich one halved marshmallow and one chocolate square. Repeat with remaining s'more ingredients.

5. Using two large scoops of cookie dough, cover entire s'more until no graham is visible. Repeat until all dough and s'mores have been used. Transfer to prepared baking sheets and refrigerate at least 15 minutes.

6. Bake until lightly golden, 12 to 14 minutes. Let cool 10 minutes before serving.

CINNAMON ROLL COOKIES

TOTAL TIME: 55 MIN / MAKES 40

We tried rolling these cookies from a log of premade sugar cookie dough and failed BADLY. Mixing up your own dough takes almost no time and makes the rolling process a thousand times easier. And those mesmerizing swirls only look intimidating—anyone can pull them off.

3 cups all-purpose flour, plus more for dusting

1 teaspoon baking powder

1 teaspoon kosher salt

1 cup (2 sticks) butter, softened

1 cup granulated sugar

1 large egg

1 tablespoon milk

1 teaspoon pure vanilla extract

FOR THE FILLING

¼ cup packed brown sugar

2 teaspoons ground cinnamon

2 tablespoons melted butter

FOR THE GLAZE

1¼ cups powdered sugar

2 tablespoons milk

1. Preheat oven to 350°F and line two baking sheets with parchment paper.

2. In a medium bowl, whisk together flour, baking powder, and salt.

3. In a large bowl using a hand mixer, beat butter and sugar until light and fluffy. Add egg, milk, and vanilla and beat until incorporated, then add dry ingredients and beat until combined. Divide dough in half.

4. On a floured surface, roll each piece of dough into a 9×10-inch rectangle, about ¼ inch thick.

5. Make filling: In small bowl, stir together brown sugar and cinnamon. Brush dough rectangles with melted butter and sprinkle with cinnamon-sugar mixture. Starting from long side closest to you, tightly roll up each rectangle into a log.

6. Slice each log into ½-inch-thick slices and transfer to prepared baking sheets, spacing cookies 1 inch apart.

7. Bake until lightly golden, 12 to 14 minutes. Let cool completely. Repeat with remaining dough.

8. Make glaze: In a small bowl, whisk together powdered sugar and milk. Drizzle glaze over cookies.

GLUTEN-FREE CHOCOLATE CHIP COOKIES

TOTAL TIME: 1 HR / MAKES 32

This is Jo's favorite chocolate chip cookie. Period. Which says a lot, considering the dough uses a combo of almond flour and cornstarch. We make sure to have a batch in the freezer ready to bake off at all times—you'll want to do the same.

2¾ cups almond flour

½ cup cornstarch

½ teaspoon baking soda

¾ teaspoon kosher salt

¾ cup (1½ sticks) melted butter, cooled

½ cup packed brown sugar

½ cup granulated sugar

2 large eggs

2 teaspoons pure vanilla extract

1¼ cups semisweet chocolate chips

1. In a medium bowl, whisk together almond flour, cornstarch, baking soda, and salt.

2. In a large bowl, whisk together melted butter and sugars until smooth. Add eggs and vanilla and whisk until smooth and slightly thickened. Add dry ingredients to wet ingredients and mix until just combined, then fold in chocolate chips.

3. Cover dough with plastic wrap and refrigerate at least 30 minutes and up to 2 days.

4. When ready to bake, preheat oven to 375°F and line two large baking sheets with parchment paper.

5. Using a medium cookie scoop, scoop balls of dough (about 1½ tablespoons each) onto prepared baking sheets, spacing cookies 2 inches apart.

6. Bake until edges are golden and center is just set, 10 to 12 minutes. Repeat with remaining dough.

BUTTER PECAN COOKIES

TOTAL TIME: 1 HR / MAKES 30

Feel like butter pecan ice cream is a totally underrated flavor? SAME. The maple syrup–infused buttercream makes these cookies stupidly addictive and special enough for any dessert spread.

1 cup (2 sticks) butter, softened

1 cup packed brown sugar

½ cup granulated sugar

2 large eggs

2 teaspoons pure vanilla extract

2 cups all-purpose flour

½ teaspoon baking soda

¼ teaspoon kosher salt

2 cups chopped pecans, divided

FOR THE MAPLE FROSTING

1 cup (2 sticks) butter, softened

3 cups powdered sugar, plus more if needed

⅓ cup heavy cream

¼ cup maple syrup

1. Preheat oven to 350°F and line two large baking sheets with parchment paper.

2. In a large bowl using a hand mixer, beat butter and sugars until light and fluffy. Add eggs, one at time, and beat until incorporated, then add vanilla. Add flour, baking soda, and salt and mix until just combined, then fold in 1 cup of chopped pecans.

3. Using a medium cookie scoop, scoop balls of dough (about 1½ tablespoons each) onto prepared baking sheets, spacing cookies 1 inch apart. Refrigerate 10 minutes.

4. Bake until golden, 10 to 12 minutes. Let cool on racks 10 minutes, then transfer to wire racks to cool completely. Repeat with remaining dough.

5. Make frosting: In a large bowl using a hand mixer, beat butter until smooth and fluffy. Add powdered sugar and beat until combined, then add heavy cream and maple syrup and beat until creamy. (If frosting is too thin, beat in more powdered sugar, ¼ cup at a time.)

6. Frost cookies and decorate with remaining 1 cup chopped pecans.

LEVAIN KNOCKOFF CHOCOLATE CHIP COOKIES

TOTAL TIME: 2 HR 30 MIN (INCLUDES CHILLING) /
MAKES 8 MASSIVE COOKIES

When someone's having a bad day at Delish, one of us volunteers to walk the seventeen blocks uptown to New York City's Levain Bakery— famous for their colossal cookies, ultra-gooey in the center and crispy outside. We baked no fewer than twenty batches to try to match their perfection, and we have to admit that we got pretttty close.

2 cups all-purpose flour

1¼ cups cake flour

2 teaspoons baking powder

¼ teaspoon baking soda

¼ teaspoon kosher salt

1 cup (2 sticks) very cold butter, cubed

⅔ cup packed brown sugar

⅔ cup granulated sugar

2 cups dark chocolate chips

1 cup very coarsely chopped walnuts, lightly toasted

2 large eggs, lightly beaten

1. Line two large baking sheets with parchment paper.

2. In a medium bowl, whisk together flours, baking powder, baking soda, and salt.

3. In a large bowl using a hand mixer, beat butter on low speed until cubes lose half their shape, 30 to 45 seconds. Add sugars and beat 30 to 60 seconds more. Add chocolate and walnuts and beat until combined.

4. Gradually add dry ingredients to wet ingredients and beat until combined. (Mixture will be a bit crumbly.) Add eggs and beat until incorporated.

5. Portion large balls of dough, about ¾ cup each. Place 4 balls of dough onto each prepared baking sheet and freeze 1 hour 30 minutes.

6. When ready to bake, preheat oven to 375°F. Place an empty baking sheet upside-down in oven and place one pan of frozen dough on top. Bake until tops are golden, about 26 minutes. Repeat with second pan of frozen dough.

These bake for double the amount of time of most cookies: Placing them on an **INVERTED BAKING SHEET** ensures the outsides don't burn.

MIX-INS TO TRY

- 1 cup white chocolate chips
- 1 cup semisweet chocolate chips
- 1 cup chopped pretzels
- 1 cup chopped soft caramels
- ½ cup toasted peanuts
- Flaky sea salt

MICHAEL STRAHAN & SARA HAINES'S
CHOCOLATE CHIP PRETZEL COOKIE

TOTAL TIME: 40 MIN / MAKES 24

When trying to establish our *ultimate* chocolate chip cookie (see page 21), the food editors duked it out live on *Strahan and Sara*. The audience chose Makinze's, but we still have a sweet spot for the hosts' creation.

1 cup (2 sticks) butter, softened

1¼ cups packed dark brown sugar

½ cup granulated sugar

1 large egg

1 large egg yolk

1 teaspoon pure vanilla extract

2 cups all-purpose flour

1 cup old-fashioned rolled oats

½ teaspoon baking soda

½ teaspoon kosher salt

¼ teaspoon ground cinnamon

1. Preheat the oven to 325°F and line two large baking sheets with parchment paper.

2. In the bowl of a stand mixer fitted with the paddle attachment, beat butter and sugars until smooth. Add egg, egg yolk, and vanilla and beat until incorporated.

3. Add flour, oats, baking soda, kosher salt, and cinnamon and beat until just combined. Fold in mix-ins.

4. Using a medium scoop, scoop balls of dough (about 1½ tablespoons each) onto prepared baking sheets, spacing cookies 2 inches apart. Sprinkle tops with flaky salt, if desired. Bake until golden, 11 to 14 minutes.

APPLE CRISP COOKIE CUPS

TOTAL TIME: 50 MIN / MAKES 18

The cutest fall dessert ever—practically made for post-apple-picking. The oatmeal cookie cup is the perfect vessel for apples sautéed in nutmeg and cinnamon and drizzled with caramel.

Cooking spray

1 cup (2 sticks) plus 2 tablespoons butter, softened, divided

1¼ cups packed brown sugar, divided

¾ cup granulated sugar, divided

2 large eggs

1 teaspoon pure vanilla extract

1¾ cups old-fashioned rolled oats

1¼ cups all-purpose flour

1 teaspoon baking powder

1 teaspoon ground cinnamon, divided

½ teaspoon kosher salt

4 Granny Smith apples, peeled, cored, and finely chopped

1½ teaspoons cornstarch

½ teaspoon ground nutmeg

Caramel sauce

1. Preheat oven to 350°F and grease two muffin tins with cooking spray.

2. In a large bowl using a hand mixer, beat 1 cup of butter, 1 cup of brown sugar, and ½ cup of granulated sugar until light and fluffy. Add eggs, one at a time, and beat until incorporated, then add vanilla. Add oats, flour, baking powder, ½ teaspoon of cinnamon, and salt and mix until just combined.

3. Using a medium cookie scoop, scoop balls of dough (about 1½ tablespoons each) into prepared muffin tin cups and press with your fingers to flatten.

4. Bake until cookies are golden and set, 18 to 20 minutes.

5. Grease the bottom of a small shot glass with cooking spray and, while cookies are still warm, press into center of each cookie to form a cup. Let cool in pans 15 minutes, then transfer to wire racks to cool completely.

6. Meanwhile, in a medium skillet over medium-high heat, melt remaining 2 tablespoons butter. Add apples and cook until beginning to soften. Stir in remaining ¼ cup each brown sugar and granulated sugar, cornstarch, nutmeg, and remaining ½ teaspoon cinnamon and cook until soft and caramelized.

7. Spoon apple filling into cups and drizzle with caramel.

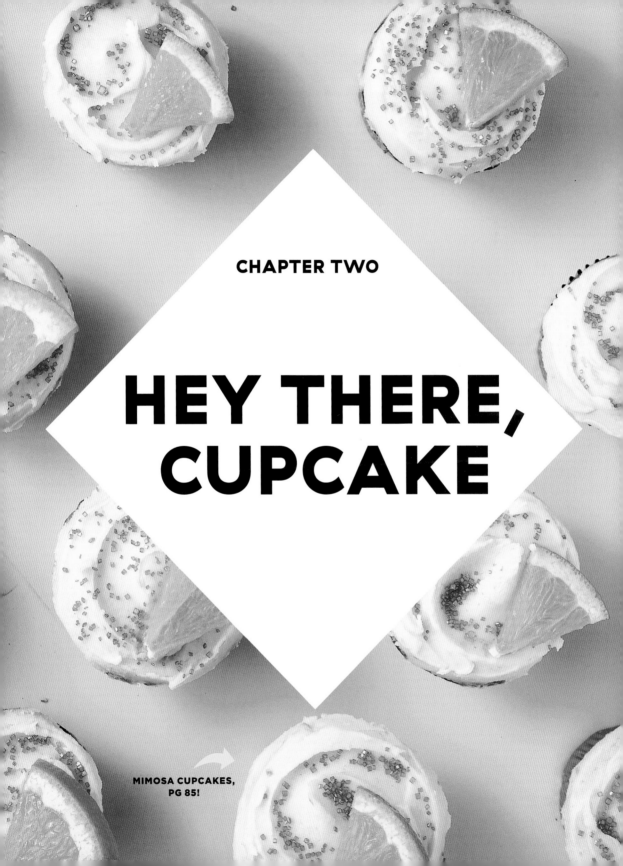

CHAPTER TWO

HEY THERE, CUPCAKE

MIMOSA CUPCAKES,
PG 85!

This cupcake batter doubles as a mean **BIRTHDAY CAKE**. Simply divide the batter between two 8-inch round pans and bake until a toothpick inserted into the center of the cakes comes out clean, about 25 minutes.

PERFECT VANILLA CUPCAKES

TOTAL TIME: 45 MIN / MAKES 16

When food assistant Makinze realized that Delish didn't have a classic cupcake recipe, she made it her business to develop one that puts others to shame. Adding a little cornstarch to the batter helps give the cake a ridiculously moist—ugh, the worst word—texture.

FOR THE CUPCAKES

2 cups all-purpose flour

3 tablespoons cornstarch

1½ teaspoons baking powder

1 teaspoon kosher salt

1 cup (2 sticks) butter, softened

1½ cups granulated sugar

3 large eggs

1 tablespoon pure vanilla extract

¾ cup milk

FOR THE FROSTING

1 cup (2 sticks) butter, softened

4 cups powdered sugar

3 to 4 tablespoons heavy cream

1 teaspoon pure vanilla extract

Pinch kosher salt

Rainbow nonpareils

1. Make cupcakes: Preheat oven to 350°F and line two muffin tins with 16 cupcake liners.

2. In a medium bowl, whisk together flour, cornstarch, baking powder, and salt.

3. In a large bowl using a hand mixer, beat butter and sugar until light and fluffy. Add eggs, one at a time, and beat until incorporated, then add vanilla. Add half the dry ingredients and beat until combined, then beat in milk. Add remaining dry ingredients and mix until just combined.

4. Fill cupcake liners three-quarters full with batter. Bake until lightly golden on top and a toothpick inserted into center of each cupcake comes out clean, about 25 minutes. Let cupcakes cool in pans 5 to 10 minutes, then transfer to a wire rack to cool completely.

5. Make frosting: In a large bowl using a hand mixer, beat butter until light and fluffy. Add powdered sugar, then add 3 tablespoons of heavy cream, vanilla, and salt and beat until smooth. If frosting is too thick, add remaining tablespoon of heavy cream.) Transfer frosting to a piping bag fitted with a large round tip.

6. Pipe frosting onto cupcakes and sprinkle with nonpareils.

KAHLÚA CHOCOLATE CUPCAKES

You don't have to love Kahlúa, the coffee-flavored rum liqueur, to love these cupcakes. But you do need to love chocolate: They're not messing around.

FOR THE CUPCAKES

1 (15-ounce) box devil's food cake mix

3 large eggs

¾ cup brewed coffee

⅓ cup vegetable oil

¼ cup Kahlúa

FOR THE FROSTING

1½ cups (3 sticks) butter, softened

4 cups powdered sugar

½ cup unsweetened cocoa powder

1 teaspoon pure vanilla extract

Pinch kosher salt

¼ cup heavy cream

1 tablespoon Kahlúa

Chocolate shavings, for garnish

Chocolate-covered espresso beans, for garnish

1. Make cupcakes: Preheat oven to 350°F and line two muffin tins with cupcake liners.

2. In a large bowl, whisk together cake mix, eggs, coffee, oil, and Kahlúa until fully incorporated.

3. Fill cupcake liners three-quarters full with batter. Bake until a toothpick inserted into center of each cupcake comes out clean, about 25 minutes. Let cool in pans 5 to 10 minutes, then transfer to a wire rack to cool completely.

4. Make frosting: In a large bowl using a hand mixer, beat butter, powdered sugar, cocoa powder, vanilla, and salt until smooth. Add heavy cream and Kahlúa and beat until fully incorporated. Transfer to a large piping bag fitted with a large closed star tip.

5. Pipe frosting onto cooled cupcakes, then garnish with espresso beans and chocolate shavings.

If you wanna make the cupcakes from scratch, follow the cupcake recipe from our **CHRISTMAS LIGHT CUPCAKES**, page 224.

S'MORES CUPCAKES

Toasted marshmallows serve as the frosting here, which is genius.
But we almost burned the Delish kitchen down trying to test these.
We first tried to broil the marshmallow-topped cupcakes, but they
caught on fire; panic ensued and lumps of charred goo emerged
from the oven. We ultimately found a better way (below).

FOR THE CUPCAKES

1 (15-ounce) box devil's
food cake mix, plus
ingredients called for
on box

3 cups graham cracker
crumbs (about 20
full graham crackers
sheets)

¾ cup (1½ sticks) melted
butter

½ cup granulated sugar

Pinch kosher salt

**FOR THE GANACHE AND
TOPPING**

1 cup semisweet
chocolate chips

½ cup heavy cream

24 marshmallows

1. Make cupcakes: Preheat oven to 350°F and line two
muffin tins with cupcake liners.

2. Prepare cake batter according to package
instructions.

3. In a small bowl, stir together graham cracker crumbs,
melted butter, granulated sugar, and salt until mixture
resembles wet sand.

4. Press about 1 tablespoon graham cracker mixture
into each cupcake liner to make mini crusts, then fill
cupcake liners three-quarters full with cake batter. Bake
until a toothpick inserted into center of each cupcake
comes out with a few moist crumbs attached, about
16 minutes. Keep the oven on.

5. Make ganache: Put chocolate chips in a large
heatproof bowl. In a small saucepan over medium
heat, heat heavy cream until steaming and bubbles
form around the edge. Pour over chocolate and let sit
5 minutes, then whisk until chocolate has completely
melted and mixture is combined.

6. Spoon about 1 tablespoon ganache onto each
cupcake, then top each with a marshmallow. Return
cupcakes to oven and bake—watching closely!—until
marshmallows are golden and very soft, 4 to 5 minutes
more.

MOSCOW MULE CUPCAKES

TOTAL TIME: 1 HR 15 MIN / MAKES 20

To make these cupcakes taste like a true Moscow mule, we discovered a genius hack: replacing the eggs, oil, and water that the box mix calls for with ginger beer for an intense flavor and perfect texture. Don't worry: the vodka's in the frosting.

FOR THE CUPCAKES

1 (15-ounce) box vanilla cake mix

1 (12-ounce) can ginger beer

½ teaspoon ground ginger

FOR THE FROSTING

1 cup (2 sticks) butter, softened

4 cups powdered sugar, divided

¼ cup vodka

1 tablespoon lime zest

2 tablespoons lime juice (about 1 lime)

20 small lime slices

20 sprigs fresh mint

1. Make cupcakes: Preheat oven to 350°F and line two muffin tins with 20 cupcake liners.

2. In a large bowl, whisk together cake mix, ginger beer, and ground ginger until fully incorporated.

3. Fill cupcake liners three-quarters full with batter. Bake until a toothpick inserted into center of each cupcake comes out clean, about 18 minutes. Let cupcakes cool in pans for 5 to 10 minutes, then transfer to a wire rack to cool completely.

4. Make frosting: In a large bowl using a hand mixer, beat butter until fluffy. Add 3 cups of powdered sugar and beat until smooth, then add vodka, lime zest, and lime juice and beat until incorporated. Add remaining 1 cup powdered sugar and beat until smooth. Transfer to a piping bag fitted with large open star tip.

5. Pipe frosting onto cooled cupcakes and garnish each with a slice of lime and sprig of mint.

BOOZY FROSTING has a tendency to break. Adding a cup of powdered sugar at the end helps ensure that the texture is nice and creamy.

MIMOSA CUPCAKES

TOTAL TIME: 1 HR 30 MIN / MAKES 18

Out-cute yourself at brunch by showing up with a batch of these instead of OJ and prosecco. Bubbly (any variety works) goes into both the batter and the frosting, so these cupcakes will definitely cure the Sunday scaries.

FOR THE CUPCAKES

1 (15-ounce) box vanilla cake mix

1 cup champagne

⅓ cup vegetable oil

3 large eggs

1 teaspoon orange zest

FOR THE CHAMPAGNE FROSTING

1 cup (2 sticks) butter, softened

4 cups powdered sugar, divided

¼ cup champagne or prosecco, at room temperature

1 teaspoon pure vanilla extract

1 teaspoon orange zest

Pinch kosher salt

Gold sanding sugar, for garnish

Orange wedges, for garnish

1. Make cupcakes: Preheat oven to 350°F and line two muffin tins with 18 cupcake liners.

2. In a large bowl, beat cake mix with champagne, oil, eggs, and orange zest.

3. Fill cupcake liners three-quarters full with batter, then bake until a toothpick inserted into center of each cupcake comes out clean, about 18 minutes. Let cool in pans 5 to 10 minutes, then transfer to a wire rack to cool completely.

4. Make frosting: In a large bowl using a hand mixer, beat butter and 2 cups of powdered sugar until fluffy. Add champagne, vanilla, orange zest, and salt and beat until incorporated, then add remaining 2 cups powdered sugar and beat until smooth and fluffy.

5. Using a small offset spatula, frost cooled cupcakes. Garnish with gold sanding sugar and an orange wedge before serving.

 Got **LEFTOVER CHAMPAGNE**? These cupcakes are the perfect way to use it up.

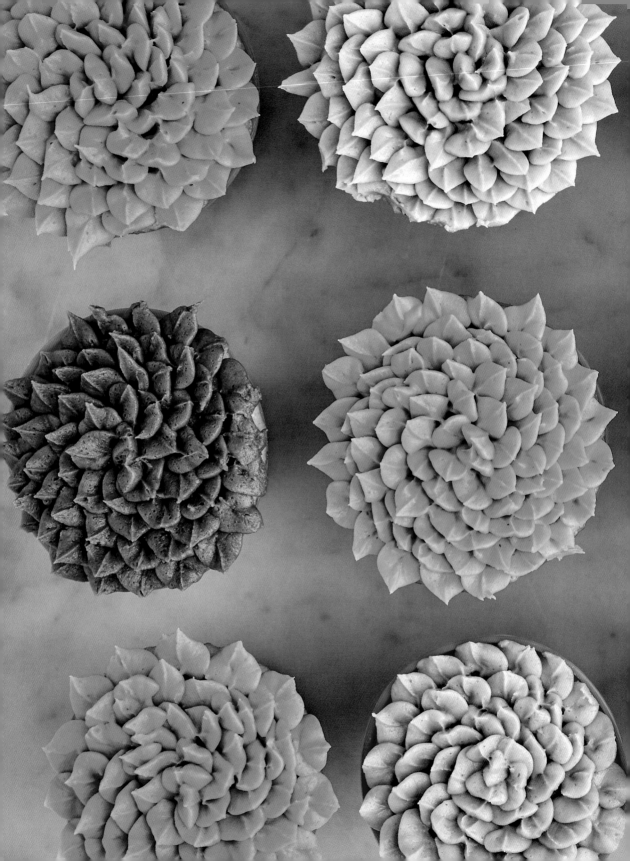

SUCCULENT CUPCAKES

TOTAL TIME: 1 HR 45 MIN / MAKES 24

When these started taking over our Pinterest feed, we were too obsessed to not try the technique ourselves. If you're the least bit comfortable handling a piping bag, you totally got this. You can find the mini silicone terra-cotta pots at most craft stores or online.

1 (15-ounce) box vanilla cake mix, plus ingredients called for on box

FOR THE FROSTING

1 cup (2 sticks) butter, softened

4 cups powdered sugar

1 teaspoon pure vanilla extract

¼ cup heavy cream

Pinch kosher salt

Green, brown, blue, yellow, and violet food coloring

24 flower pot cupcake molds

1. Preheat oven to 350° and line two muffin tins with 24 cupcake liners.

2. Prepare cake batter according to package instructions. Fill cupcake liners three-quarters full with batter. Bake until a toothpick inserted into center of each cupcake comes out clean, about 20 minutes.

3. Let cupcakes cool in pans 5 to 10 minutes, then transfer to a wire rack to completely. Place cooled cupcakes in terra-cotta pots.

RECIPE CONTINUES

4. Make frosting: In a large bowl using a hand mixer, beat butter until light and fluffy. Add powdered sugar and beat until smooth, then add vanilla, heavy cream, and salt and beat until fluffy. Divide frosting among three bowls. To make forest green, use 3 drops green food coloring and 1 drop brown. To make bright green, use 2 drops blue food coloring and 1 drop yellow. To make purple, use 2 drops violet food coloring. Transfer frosting to three piping bags fitted with leaf tips.

5. Pipe leaves around edge of cupcake, slightly overlapping each other. Pipe another circle of leaves within first circle, letting them slightly fall over the first. Continue until cupcake is completely frosted. Repeat with remaining frosting and cupcakes.

The **LEAF TIP** is essential for creating the succulent look. When piping, hold your bag at a slight upward angle, squeeze hard to form the base of the leaf, then slowly pull the tip upward as you squeeze to give the leaf some lift.

NEAPOLITAN CUPCAKES

TOTAL TIME: 30 MIN / MAKES 30

These layered–ice cream–inspired cupcakes are for the days when you can't commit to Team Chocolate or Team Vanilla. But the real reason to make them is the strawberry cream cheese frosting, which you'll definitely be eating with a spoon.

FOR THE CUPCAKES

1 (15-ounce) box vanilla cake mix, plus ingredients called for on box

1 (15-ounce) box devil's food cake mix, plus ingredients called for on box

FOR THE STRAWBERRY FROSTING

1 (8-ounce) block cream cheese, softened

4 tablespoons (½ stick) butter, softened

¼ cup strawberry jam

3 cups powdered sugar

1 to 2 tablespoons heavy cream

1 teaspoon pure vanilla extract

4 drops pink food coloring

Pinch kosher salt

1. Make cupcakes: Preheat oven to 350°F and line two muffin tins with cupcake liners.

2. Prepare both cake batters according to package instructions, then fill cupcake liners three-quarters full, half with chocolate batter and half with vanilla batter. Bake until a toothpick inserted into center of each cupcake comes out clean, about 20 minutes. Let cool in pans 5 to 10 minutes, then transfer to a wire rack to cool completely. Line a muffin tin with six more liners, and repeat with remaining batter.

3. Make frosting: In a large bowl using a hand mixer, beat cream cheese and butter until light and fluffy, then beat in strawberry preserves. Add powdered sugar and beat until combined, then add 1 tablespoon of heavy cream, vanilla, food coloring, and salt and beat until smooth. Beat in remaining 1 tablespoon of heavy cream if frosting seems too thick. Transfer frosting to a piping bag fitted with a large round tip.

4. Pipe frosting onto cooled cupcakes.

CINNAMON TOAST CRUNCH CUPCAKES

TOTAL TIME: 1 HR 20 MIN / MAKES 24

At Delish, we never show up to a meeting empty-handed.
CTC is one of those kid cereals that adults can still fully get behind,
so we knew a batch of these would be the way to a group of
grown men's hearts (looking at you, Brian).

FOR THE CUPCAKES

1 box vanilla cake mix,
    plus ingredients called
    for on box

1 teaspoon ground
    cinnamon

¼ cup cinnamon sugar

FOR THE FROSTING

1¼ cups (2½ sticks)
    butter, softened

3¾ cups powdered sugar

1¼ teaspoons pure
    vanilla extract

¾ teaspoon ground
    cinnamon

Pinch kosher salt

3 to 4 tablespoons heavy
    cream

Cinnamon Toast Crunch,
    for garnish

1. Make cupcakes: Preheat oven to 350°F and line two muffin tins with cupcake liners.

2. Prepare cake mix according to package instructions, then whisk in cinnamon.

3. Fill cupcake liners with 1 tablespoon batter, then sprinkle with a layer of cinnamon-sugar. Repeat layering, then top with 1 tablespoon more batter. Bake until lightly golden on top and a toothpick inserted into center of each cupcake comes out clean, about 20 minutes. Let cool in pans 5 to 10 minutes, then transfer to a wire rack to cool completely.

4. Make frosting: In a large bowl using a hand mixer, beat butter until light and fluffy. Add powdered sugar, vanilla, cinnamon, and salt and beat until combined. Gradually add heavy cream, one tablespoon at a time, until creamy. Transfer frosting to a piping bag fitted with a large round tip.

5. Pipe frosting onto cooled cupcakes. Garnish with Cinnamon Toast Crunch before serving.

OWL CUPCAKES

TOTAL TIME: 1 HR 20 MIN / MAKES 24

File these under Cutest. Cupcake. Ever. Also, easiest ever: This is a great baking project for kids. All you need are Oreo halves and mini M&Ms to create the owl's larger-than-life eyes.

FOR THE CUPCAKES

1 (15-ounce) box devil's food cake mix, plus ingredients called for on box

1 (3.9-ounce) box instant chocolate pudding

1¼ cups whole milk

½ cup vegetable oil

3 large eggs

FOR THE FROSTING

½ cup (1 stick) melted butter

3 cups powdered sugar

1 cup unsweetened cocoa powder

¼ teaspoon kosher salt

¼ cup whole milk

1 teaspoon pure vanilla extract

FOR TOPPING

24 Oreos, halves separated

48 chocolate mini M&Ms

24 orange mini M&Ms

1. Make cupcakes: Preheat oven to 350°F and line two muffin tins with cupcake liners.

2. In a large bowl, whisk together cake mix, pudding mix, milk, oil, and eggs until incorporated.

3. Fill cupcake liners three-quarters full with batter. Bake until a toothpick inserted into center of each cupcake comes out clean, 18 to 21 minutes. Let cool in pans 5 to 10 minutes, then transfer to a wire rack to cool completely.

4. Make frosting: In a large bowl, whisk together melted butter, powdered sugar, cocoa powder, and salt. Add milk and vanilla and whisk until smooth.

5. Using the bottom of a spoon, frost cooled cupcakes, making two swooshes on top for ears.

6. Top with Oreo halves, creme-side up, for eyes. Dot the bottom of chocolate mini M&Ms with frosting and place on top of Oreo halves for eyeballs. Place an orange mini M&M for the nose.

A party without
cupcakes is called
a meeting.

CANNOLI CUPCAKES

TOTAL TIME: 1 HR 35 MIN / MAKES 24

Real talk: The filling of a cannoli is the best part, which is exactly why these cupcakes are so amazing—they're stuffed with it. Spooning some melted chocolate on top provides the perfect balance.

1 (15-ounce box) vanilla cake mix, plus ingredients called for on box

1 cup (2 sticks) butter, softened

2 (8-ounce) blocks cream cheese, softened

1 cup whole-milk ricotta

6 cups powdered sugar

2 teaspoons pure vanilla extract

½ teaspoon ground cinnamon

½ teaspoon kosher salt

⅔ cup mini chocolate chips

1 cup semisweet chocolate chips, melted

2 tablespoons coconut oil

1. Preheat oven to 350°F and line two muffin tins with cupcake liners.

2. Prepare cake batter according to package instructions. Divide batter among cupcake liners and bake until a toothpick inserted into center of each cupcake comes out clean, about 20 minutes. Let cool completely.

3. Meanwhile, in a large bowl using a hand mixer, beat butter, cream cheese, and ricotta until fluffy. Add powdered sugar, vanilla, cinnamon, and salt and beat until smooth. Fold in mini chocolate chips. Transfer frosting to a large pastry bag fitted with a large tip.

4. Using a teaspoon, scoop out middle of each cupcake to create a small well. Pipe frosting inside well and on top of each cupcake.

5. In a small bowl, stir together melted chocolate and coconut oil until smooth. Spoon over frosting. Let set slightly before serving.

DOLE WHIP CUPCAKES

TOTAL TIME: 1 HR 40 MIN / MAKES 24

Disney diehards all beeline for the theme parks' classic pineapple soft serve as quickly as they can, so we created these cupcakes for all of them. The pineapple-laced cake batter and frosting are next-level.

FOR THE CUPCAKES

1 (15-ounce) box yellow cake mix

1 cup crushed pineapple with juice

⅓ cup vegetable oil

3 large eggs

FOR THE FROSTING

1 cup (2 sticks) butter, softened

4 cups powdered sugar

¼ cup pineapple juice

1 teaspoon pure vanilla extract

24 small pineapple wedges, for garnish

1. Make cupcakes: Preheat oven to 325°F and line two muffin tins with cupcake liners.

2. In a large bowl using a hand mixer, beat cake mix, crushed pineapple and juice, oil, and eggs until combined, 2 minutes.

3. Fill cupcake liners three-quarters full with batter, then bake until a toothpick inserted into center of each cupcake comes out clean, 20 to 22 minutes. Let cupcakes cool in pans 5 to 10 minutes, then transfer to a wire rack to cool completely.

4. Meanwhile, make frosting: In a large bowl using a hand mixer, beat butter, 2 cups of powdered sugar, pineapple juice, and vanilla until smooth. Add remaining 2 cups powdered sugar and beat until light and fluffy. Transfer frosting to a piping bag fitted with a ½-inch star tip.

5. Swirl frosting onto cooled cupcakes. Garnish each with a pineapple wedge and a cut decorative straw before serving.

BOSTON CREAM CUPCAKES

TOTAL TIME: 1 HR 30 MIN / MAKES 24

Anyone who loves Boston cream pie knows it's not pie at all—it's a spongy vanilla cake. We swap out making a homemade pastry cream for mixing up store-bought vanilla pudding mix, which gets sandwiched between the cupcake layers. Heaven in a bite.

FOR THE CUPCAKES

2 cups all-purpose flour

3 tablespoons cornstarch

1½ teaspoons baking powder

1 teaspoon kosher salt

1 cup (2 sticks) butter, softened

1½ cups granulated sugar

3 large eggs

1 tablespoon pure vanilla extract

¾ cup whole milk

FOR THE FILLING

2 cups whole milk

1 (3.4-ounce) box instant vanilla pudding mix

FOR THE GANACHE

1½ cups semisweet chocolate chips

¾ cup heavy cream

1. Make cupcakes: Preheat oven to 350°F and line two muffin tins with cupcake liners.

2. In a medium bowl, whisk together flour, cornstarch, baking powder, and salt.

3. In a large bowl using a hand mixer, beat butter and sugar until light and fluffy. Add eggs, one at a time, and beat until incorporated, then add vanilla. Add half the dry ingredients to the wet ingredients and beat until combined, then add milk and beat until incorporated. Add remaining dry ingredients and beat until just combined.

4. Fill cupcake liners three-quarters full with batter. Bake until lightly golden on top and a toothpick inserted into center of each cupcake comes out clean, about 25 minutes. Let cool completely.

5. Make filling: In a small bowl, whisk together milk and pudding mix, then let stand until thick, 3 minutes.

6. Make ganache: Put chocolate chips in a large heatproof bowl. In a small saucepan over medium heat, heat heavy cream until steaming. Pour cream over chocolate and let sit 5 minutes, then whisk until chocolate has completely melted.

7. Cut each cupcake in half crosswise. Spoon filling onto cupcake bottoms and sandwich with cupcake tops. Spoon ganache over the tops.

CAKED UP CAFÉ

NEW YORK

AT ANY given time, there are nearly two dozen varieties of cupcakes behind the glass case at Caked Up Café. They're all to die for, but if the Maple Bacon Cupcakes aren't part of the line-up, owner Denis Byrnes won't hear the end of it from customers. "We have to have it every day," she laughs about the bestseller. (Instagram is proof of this: You can't scroll through a grid of geotagged posts without seeing one—or four—pop up.) The idea for the cupcake came about honestly. "During brunch one day, it dawned on us. What if we made pancakes and bacon into this perfect little bite," Denise says. The cupcake batter is spiked with maple syrup and buttermilk, and when it's baked, it tastes like the fluffiest, lightest cupcake you've ever had. On top of it sit two actual silver dollar pancakes, drenched in maple syrup, topped off with a pat of butter, and surrounded by tiny pieces of bacon. You can call it a cupcake if you want—but we're calling it our excuse to eat dessert for breakfast.

MAPLE BACON CUPCAKES

TOTAL TIME: 50 MIN / SERVES: 18

¾ cup granulated sugar

¾ cup buttermilk

¼ cup (½ stick) salted butter, softened

¼ cup vegetable oil

2 large eggs

2 teaspoons vanilla extract

1 ¾ cup all-purpose flour

2 teaspoons baking powder

½ cup maple syrup, plus more for drizzling

36 mini pancakes

6 slices cooked bacon, chopped

18 tiny butter squares

FOR THE FROSTING

2 ½ cups (5 sticks) unsalted butter, softened

2 tablespoons heavy cream

1 tablespoon vanilla

8 cups powdered sugar

1. Preheat oven to 350° and line two muffin tins with 18 cupcake liners.

2. In a large bowl, beat sugar, buttermilk, butter, oil, eggs, and vanilla until incorporated. In a separate bowl whisk together flour and baking soda.

3. Add dry ingredients to wet ingredients and beat until just combined. Stir in maple syrup.

4. Fill cupcake liners three-quarters full with batter. Bake until a toothpick inserted into the center of each cupcake comes out clean, about 20 minutes. Let cool completely.

5. Make frosting: In a large bowl using a hand mixer, beat butter, cream, and vanilla until smooth. Gradually add powdered sugar until incorporated, then beat until fluffy.

6. Using a large star tip, pipe frosting onto cupcakes. Top with pancakes and a tiny butter square, then press bacon bits around sides. Drizzle with more syrup.

FRAPPUCCINO CUPCAKES

TOTAL TIME: 50 MIN / MAKES 24

The best birthday surprise for the Frapp lover in your life (we all have one). Coffee goes into both the chocolate cupcake and the frosting for serious mocha vibes. If you skip your morning cup and go straight for one of these, your secret's safe with us.

FOR THE CUPCAKES

1 box chocolate cake mix

3 large eggs

⅓ cup vegetable oil

1 cup brewed coffee

½ cup mini chocolate chips

FOR THE FROSTING

1 cup (2 sticks) butter, softened

5 cups powdered sugar

½ cup heavy cream

¼ teaspoon espresso powder

Pinch kosher salt

Shaved chocolate, for garnish

Chocolate syrup, for garnish

Caramel sauce, for garnish

1. Make cupcakes: Preheat oven to 350°F and line two muffin tins with cupcake liners.

2. In a large bowl, beat cake mix, eggs, oil, and coffee until incorporated, then fold in chocolate chips.

3. Fill cupcake liners three-quarters full with batter. Bake until a toothpick inserted into center of each cupcake comes out clean, about 18 minutes. Let cupcakes cool in pans 5 to 10 minutes, then transfer to a wire rack to cool completely.

4. Make frosting: In a large bowl using a hand mixer, beat butter and 2½ cups of powdered sugar until smooth. Add remaining 2½ cups powdered sugar, heavy cream, espresso powder, and salt and beat until fluffy. Transfer frosting to a pastry bag fitted with a large closed star tip.

5. Pipe frosting onto cooled cupcakes, then sprinkle with chocolate shavings and drizzle with chocolate syrup and caramel. Garnish with a cut decorative green straw before serving.

SORTING HAT CUPCAKES

TOTAL TIME: 1 HR 20 MIN / MAKES 24

Harry Potter fans go CRAZY for these cupcakes: You stuff them with four different colors of frosting—each one reps a Hogwarts House—so once your friends take their first bite, they know whether they're truly a Gryffindor, Hufflepuff, Slytherin, or Ravenclaw.

1 (15-ounce) box white cake mix, plus ingredients called for on box

FOR THE SORTING HATS

¼ cup semisweet chocolate chips, melted

24 Hershey's Kisses

12 Oreos, creme filling removed

FOR THE FROSTING

1½ cups (3 sticks) butter, softened

6 cups powdered sugar

¼ cup heavy cream, plus more if needed

2 tablespoons butterscotch syrup

Pinch kosher salt

Red, yellow, green, and blue food coloring

Gold sprinkles, for garnish

1. Preheat oven to 350°F and line two muffin tins with 24 cupcake liners.

2. Prepare cake batter according to package instructions, then fill cupcake liners three-quarters full with batter. Bake until a toothpick inserted into center of each cupcake comes out clean, 20 to 25 minutes. Let cool completely.

3. Make sorting hats: Spread melted chocolate onto bottoms of Hershey's Kisses and press onto Oreo halves.

4. Make frosting: In a large bowl using a hand mixer, beat butter until fluffy. Add powdered sugar, heavy cream, butterscotch, and salt and beat until smooth.

5. Divide all but ⅓ cup frosting among four bowls. Using food coloring, dye one bowl each red, yellow, green, and blue.

6. Using a teaspoon, scoop a well in center of each cooled cupcake, then fill with a different color.

7. Transfer remaining white buttercream to a piping bag fitted with a large round tip. Pipe frosting onto cupcakes and garnish with gold sprinkles and Sorting Hats.

CHEESECAKE-STUFFED CUPCAKES

TOTAL TIME: 1 HR 40 MIN / MAKES 24

After stuffing cookies with cheesecake (see page 17), we knew we needed to try the technique with cupcakes, too (we're cheesecake maniacs, OK?!). Let's just say these'll blow your mind.

1 (15-ounce) box devil's food cake mix, plus ingredients called for on box

FOR THE FILLING

2 (8-ounce) blocks cream cheese, softened

½ cup powdered sugar

2 large eggs

1 teaspoon pure vanilla extract

Pinch kosher salt

4 tablespoons rainbow sprinkles, divided

FOR THE FROSTING

1 cup (2 sticks) butter, softened

2½ cups powdered sugar

¾ cup unsweetened cocoa powder

2 teaspoons pure vanilla extract

Pinch kosher salt

¼ cup heavy cream

1. Preheat oven to 350°F and line two muffin tins with 24 cupcake liners.

2. Prepare cake batter according to package instructions.

3. Make filling: In a large bowl using a hand mixer, beat cream cheese and powdered sugar until smooth. Add eggs, vanilla, and salt and beat until combined. Fold in 2 tablespoons sprinkles.

4. Fill cupcake liners half full with cake batter, then drop 1 teaspoon cheesecake filling into each. Bake until a toothpick inserted into center of each cupcake comes out clean, about 20 minutes. Let cool in pans 5 to 10 minutes, then transfer to a wire rack to cool completely.

5. Meanwhile, make frosting: In a large bowl using a hand mixer, beat butter until light and fluffy. Add powdered sugar, cocoa powder, vanilla, and salt and beat until fully incorporated. Add heavy cream and beat until smooth. Transfer frosting to a piping bag fitted with a large round tip.

6. Pipe frosting onto cupcakes and garnish with remaining 2 tablespoons rainbow sprinkles before serving.

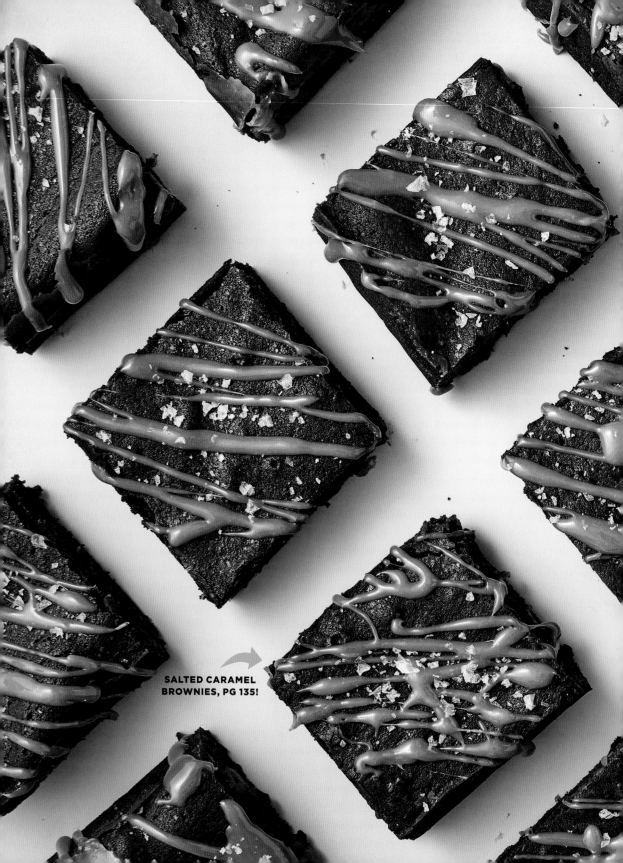

SALTED CARAMEL BROWNIES, PG 135!

CHAPTER THREE

BROWNIE POINTS

BEST-EVER BROWNIES

TOTAL TIME: 40 MIN / MAKES 15

We take brownies very seriously—so seriously that we are NOT JOKING when we say this is the only recipe you'll ever need. It checks all the boxes: unbelievably fudgy, intensely crackly top, chewy corners of perfection.

1 cup (2 sticks) butter, cut into 1-inch pieces, plus more for pan

1¼ cups all-purpose flour

¼ cup unsweetened cocoa powder

1 teaspoon kosher salt

2 cups semisweet chocolate chips, divided

1½ cups granulated sugar

½ cup packed brown sugar

5 large eggs

2 teaspoons pure vanilla extract

Flaky sea salt (optional)

1. Preheat oven to 350°F. Butter a 9×13-inch pan and line with parchment paper.

2. In a medium bowl, whisk together flour, cocoa powder, and salt.

3. Set a large heatproof bowl over a saucepan of barely simmering water to create a double boiler. Place butter and 1½ cups of chocolate chips in bowl and heat, stirring occasionally, until completely melted.

4. Remove bowl from heat, then whisk in sugars until combined. Add eggs, one at a time, and whisk until incorporated, then add vanilla. Stir dry ingredients into chocolate mixture until just combined, then fold in remaining ½ cup chocolate chips.

5. Pour batter into prepared pan and bake until a toothpick inserted into center comes out with a few moist crumbs attached, about 30 minutes.

6. Let cool completely in pan before slicing and sprinkling with sea salt, if using.

If you normally ignore the suggestion to use **ROOM-TEMPERATURE EGGS**, you gotta follow it here. Cold eggs can make the chocolate seize.

BAILEYS BROWNIES

Just look at these stunners. The boozy sweetened
condensed milk topping is more fudge than frosting,
and we are here for it.

Cooking spray

1 (18.3-ounce) box brownie mix,
plus ingredients called for on
box

1 teaspoon espresso powder

½ cup sweetened condensed milk

1¾ cups milk chocolate
chips

¼ cup Baileys Irish Cream

½ teaspoon pure vanilla
extract

Pinch kosher salt

1. Preheat oven to 350°F. Line an 8×8-inch pan with parchment paper
and grease with cooking spray.

2. Prepare brownie batter according to package instructions. Stir in
espresso powder and pour into prepared pan. Bake until a toothpick
inserted into center comes out with a few moist crumbs attached,
40 minutes. Let cool completely.

3. In a medium heatproof bowl, combine condensed milk, chocolate chips, Baileys, vanilla, and salt. Place bowl over a pot of barely
simmering water to create a double boiler and stir constantly until
chocolate is completely melted.

4. Pour chocolate mixture over cooled brownies and refrigerate until
set, 30 minutes.

5. Slice into squares and serve.

Wanna make **BROWNIES FROM SCRATCH** for this instead of using a mix? Follow our recipe on page 115 and double the fudge topping.

MINT CHOCOLATE CHIP BROWNIES

TOTAL TIME: 1 HR / MAKES 9

We bake an entire layer of Andes mints into these brownies (we crazy like that), but what turns them into absolute insanity? A thick layer of peppermint chocolate chip buttercream all over the top.

FOR THE BROWNIES
Cooking spray

¾ cup (1½ sticks) melted butter

1½ cups granulated sugar

¾ cup unsweetened cocoa powder

4 large eggs

¼ cup strong brewed coffee

1 teaspoon peppermint extract

¾ cup all-purpose flour

½ teaspoon kosher salt

28 Andes mints, plus more, chopped, for garnish

FOR THE FROSTING
½ cup (1 stick) butter, softened

3 cups powdered sugar

¼ cup milk

½ teaspoon peppermint extract

4 drops green food coloring

½ cup mini chocolate chips

1. Make brownies: Preheat oven to 350°F. Line an 8×8-inch pan with parchment paper, and grease with cooking spray.

2. In a large bowl, whisk together melted butter, sugar, and cocoa powder. Add eggs, one a time, then add coffee and peppermint extract. Add flour and salt and stir until just combined.

3. Pour batter into prepared pan and top with an even layer of Andes mints. Bake until a toothpick inserted into center comes out with a few moist crumbs attached, about 40 minutes. Let cool completely.

4. Make frosting: In a large bowl using a hand mixer, beat butter until light and fluffy. Add powdered sugar, milk, peppermint extract, and food coloring and beat until smooth, then fold in chocolate chips.

5. Spread frosting over cooled brownies in a thick, even layer. Slice into squares, then sprinkle with chopped Andes mints.

COOKIE DOUGH BROWNIES

TOTAL TIME: 1 HR / MAKES 9

If cookie dough is your love language, don't waste any more time—bake these ASAP. Each bite is equal parts fudgy brownie and creamy cookie dough. (Bonus: The cookie dough is made with almond flour, so it's totally edible raw.)

FOR THE BROWNIES
Cooking spray

¾ cup (1½ sticks) melted butter

1½ cups granulated sugar

½ cup unsweetened cocoa powder

4 large eggs

2 teaspoons pure vanilla extract

¾ cup all-purpose flour

½ teaspoon kosher salt

FOR THE COOKIE DOUGH
½ cup (1 stick) butter, softened

⅓ cup powdered sugar

1½ cups almond flour

1 teaspoon pure vanilla extract

½ teaspoon kosher salt

½ cup mini chocolate chips

1. Make brownies: Preheat oven to 350°F. Line an 8×8-inch pan with parchment paper and grease with cooking spray.

2. In a large bowl, whisk together melted butter, sugar, and cocoa powder. Add eggs, one at a time, then add vanilla. Stir in flour and salt until just combined.

3. Pour batter into prepared pan and bake until a toothpick inserted into center comes out with only a few moist crumbs attached, about 28 minutes. Let cool completely.

4. Meanwhile, make cookie dough: In a large bowl using a hand mixer, beat butter and powdered sugar until light and fluffy. Add almond flour, vanilla, and salt and beat until smooth. Fold in chocolate chips.

5. Spread cookie dough over cooled brownies in a thick, even layer. Refrigerate 20 minutes before slicing into squares and serving.

S'MORES POKE BROWNIES

TOTAL TIME: 45 MIN / MAKES 12

We're big believers in poke cakes, so why not brownies? The poke holes get filled with marshmallow creme (a Delish pantry essential, TBH) before the top gets blanketed with mini marshmallows and drizzled with warm fudge sauce. Game changer.

- 6 graham crackers, plus crushed graham crackers for garnish
- 1 (18.3-ounce) box brownie mix, plus ingredients called for on box
- 1 cup marshmallow creme
- 1½ cups mini marshmallows (about 30)

1. Preheat oven to 350°F and line an 8×8-inch pan with parchment paper.

2. Line bottom of prepared pan with graham crackers (you may need to trim some). Prepare brownie batter according to package instructions and pour into pan over graham crackers. Bake until a toothpick inserted into center comes out with a few moist crumbs attached, about 40 minutes. Let cool completely.

3. Preheat broiler.

4. Using the end of a wooden spoon, poke holes all over cooled brownie.

5. In a small heatproof bowl, microwave marshmallow creme with 1 tablespoon water on low for 15 seconds. Stir until smooth, then pour into holes in brownie. Top all over with mini marshmallows and broil until golden, 2 minutes.

6. Garnish with crushed graham crackers before slicing into squares.

More brownie fillings to try with the poke technique: **CARAMEL, CHOCOLATE SAUCE,** and **PEANUT BUTTER.**

CHOCOLATE:

IT'S

CHEAPER

THAN

THERAPY

BLACKBERRY CHEESECAKE BROWNIES

TOTAL TIME: 1 HR 15 MIN / MAKES 20

THOSE SWIRLS. To get the bright purple look, you make your own quick jam—simmer blackberries, sugar, and water on the stove for 10 minutes, kinda quick—and swirl it into the cheesecake mixture before baking.

FOR THE BLACKBERRY SAUCE

1 (6-ounce) package fresh blackberries

2 tablespoons granulated sugar

Juice of ½ lemon

FOR THE BROWNIES

Cooking spray

1 (18.3-ounce) box brownie mix, plus ingredients called for on box

2 (8-ounce) blocks cream cheese, softened

½ cup sugar

¼ cup sour cream

2 large eggs

2 teaspoons pure vanilla extract

Pinch kosher salt

1. Make blackberry sauce: In a small saucepan over medium-low heat, combine blackberries, sugar, lemon juice, and 2 tablespoons water. Cook, stirring occasionally, until blackberries have broken down, 8 to 10 minutes. Strain through a fine-mesh strainer set over a heatproof bowl and let cool slightly.

2. Make brownies: Preheat oven to 350°F. Line a 9×13-inch pan with parchment paper and grease with cooking spray.

3. Prepare brownie batter according to package instructions and pour into prepared pan.

4. In a medium bowl using a hand mixer, beat cream cheese, sugar, and sour cream until light and fluffy. Add eggs, vanilla, and salt and beat until well combined.

5. Pour cheesecake mixture over brownie batter and smooth into an even layer. Spoon dollops of blackberry sauce all over cheesecake mixture and swirl with a toothpick or knife.

6. Bake until center of cheesecake mixture is only slightly jiggly, about 35 minutes. Let cool in pan before slicing and serving.

PEANUT BUTTER COOKIE—STUFFED BROWNIES

TOTAL TIME: 1 HR / MAKES 16

Why these exist: At Delish, we're equally committed to peanut butter cookies and brownies, and wanted a way to devour both at the same time. Scoops of cookie dough bake INSIDE brownie batter, then these get drizzled with melty PB and topped with Reese's Pieces. The ultimate chocolate–peanut butter coma.

Cooking spray

1 (18.3-ounce) box brownie mix, plus ingredients called for on box

FOR THE COOKIE DOUGH

¾ cup all-purpose flour

½ teaspoon baking soda

¼ teaspoon kosher salt

4 tablespoons (½ stick) butter, softened

¼ cup granulated sugar

¼ cup packed brown sugar

1 large egg yolk

½ teaspoon pure vanilla extract

½ cup smooth peanut butter

FOR TOPPING

¼ cup melted peanut butter

¼ cup chopped Reese's Pieces

1. Preheat oven to 350°F. Line an 8×8-inch pan with parchment paper and grease with cooking spray.

2. Prepare brownie batter according to package instructions and pour into prepared pan.

3. Make cookie dough: In a medium bowl, whisk together flour, baking soda, and salt.

4. In a large bowl using a hand mixer, beat butter and sugars until light and fluffy. Add egg, vanilla, and peanut butter and beat until combined. Add dry ingredients to wet ingredients and mix until just combined.

5. Using an ice cream scoop, scoop a layer of cookie dough on top of brownie batter. Bake until a toothpick inserted into center comes out clean, about 40 minutes. Let cool slightly.

6. Drizzle with melted peanut butter and sprinkle with Reese's Pieces before slicing into squares and serving.

WE'VE GOT A SWEET SPOT

LOVEPUPPIES BROWNIES

AUSTIN, TX

JOEL HARO didn't necessarily set out to become Austin's resident brownie guy. But, as he puts it, "There are certainly worse things." After a stint in Kentucky for college, Joel returned home to Texas to start LovePuppies Brownies in 2009—but not without a nod to the birthplace of bourbon. Joel riffed on a Kentucky Screwdriver (a mix of bourbon and orange juice) to develop this dark chocolate brownie with orange liqueur and candied orange peel.

Some customers expect the throwback to Joel's college days to taste like, well, college: "For whatever reason, I think people are afraid it'll be like taking a shot of bourbon," he jokes. "That's not the case!" He spent a lot of time researching and developing flavors for that very reason—to make sure the brownie wouldn't taste like straight-up booze. The bourbon flavor itself is subtle, and complements the bitter chocolate and sweet orange.

Some of Joel's brownies rotate seasonally, but this one's always on the menu—despite its underdog status. "Honestly, I like it so much," he says, "I just keep it around."

KENTUCKY SCREWDRIVER BROWNIES

TIME 24 MIN / MAKES 55

Cooking spray

1½ cups (3 sticks) melted butter

1¼ cups unsweetened cocoa powder

8 large eggs

4 cups sugar

3¼ cups all-purpose flour

Pinch kosher salt

3 tablespoons bourbon

1 tablespoon orange liqueur

¼ cup coarsely chopped candied orange peel

¾ cup dark chocolate chips

1. Preheat oven to 350°F and grease a half sheet tray with cooking spray.

2. In a large bowl, whisk together melted butter and cocoa powder until smooth.

3. In a large bowl using a hand mixer, beat eggs and sugar until combined. Add flour, salt, bourbon, and orange liqueur and beat until well combined. Add butter-cocoa mixture and beat until just combined. Fold in candied orange peel and chocolate chips.

4. Spread batter into prepared pan and smooth top. Bake 20 minutes, rotating pan halfway through. Let cool completely before slicing into squares.

CHOCOLATE-COVERED STRAWBERRY BROWNIES

TOTAL TIME: 1 HR 25 MIN / MAKES 16

Note to my valentine: Make me these. You bake the brownies, then top them with a whole layer of strawberries before pouring over a thick, melty ganache. So much better than plain old chocolate-covered strawberries.

Cooking spray

1 (18.3-ounce) box brownie mix, plus ingredients called for on box

2⅓ cups semisweet chocolate chips

1 cup heavy cream

1½ cups halved strawberries

1. Preheat oven to 350°F. Line an 8×8-inch pan with parchment paper and grease with cooking spray.

2. Prepare brownie batter according to package instructions and pour into prepared pan. Bake until a toothpick inserted into center comes out with a few moist crumbs attached, 25 to 30 minutes. Let cool completely.

3. Put chocolate chips in a large heatproof bowl. In a small saucepan over medium heat, heat heavy cream until steaming and bubbles form around edge. Pour cream over chocolate and let sit 5 minutes, then whisk until chocolate has completely melted and mixture is combined.

4. Top cooled brownies with strawberries and pour over ganache. Refrigerate until ganache has set, about 15 minutes, then slice into squares.

SALTED CARAMEL BROWNIES

TOTAL TIME: 50 MIN / MAKES 12

For when you really want to treat yo'self (or someone you love), there's no better way than this. The homemade brownie is amazing on its own, but the real magic comes from the cheater caramel sauce: gooey, rich, and only two ingredients.

FOR THE CARAMEL

1 (11-ounce) bag caramels, unwrapped

5 tablespoons heavy cream, divided

FOR THE BROWNIES

Cooking spray

¾ cup all-purpose flour

½ teaspoon kosher salt

¾ cup (1½ sticks) melted butter

1¼ cups granulated sugar

½ cup unsweetened cocoa powder

4 large eggs

2 teaspoons pure vanilla extract

Flaky sea salt

1. Make caramel: In a small saucepan over medium-low heat, heat caramels and 3 tablespoons of heavy cream, stirring constantly, until melted, about 5 minutes.

2. Make brownies: Preheat oven to 350°F. Line a 9×9-inch pan with parchment paper and grease with cooking spray.

3. In a medium bowl, whisk together flour and salt.

4. In a large bowl, whisk together melted butter, sugar, and cocoa powder until incorporated. Add eggs, one at a time, and whisk until incorporated, then add vanilla. Gradually add dry ingredients to wet ingredients, stirring until just combined.

5. Pour half the brownie batter into prepared pan and top with all but ¼ cup of caramel. Sprinkle with flaky salt, then pour in remaining batter and smooth top.

6. Bake until a toothpick inserted into center comes out with a few moist crumbs attached, about 30 minutes. Let cool completely.

7. Return saucepan with remaining ¼ cup caramel to medium-low heat. Add remaining 2 tablespoons heavy cream to caramel and heat, stirring, until melted. Drizzle over brownies and sprinkle with flaky salt.

BIRTHDAY CAKE BLONDIES, PG 142!

CHAPTER FOUR

BLONDIES
HAVE MORE FUN

BEST-EVER BLONDIES

TOTAL TIME: 1 HR / MAKES 12

Blondies always get overlooked for brownies, which we just don't get. When you're making a classic blondie, browning the butter for its distinctive nutty flavor is a must, as is using white chocolate chips and toasted walnuts. Best topped with a scoop of vanilla ice cream.

Cooking spray

½ cup (1 stick) butter

¾ cup packed brown sugar

¼ cup granulated sugar

1 large egg

2 teaspoons pure vanilla extract

½ teaspoon kosher salt

1 cup all-purpose flour

1 cup white chocolate chips

½ cup chopped toasted walnuts

Ice cream, for serving (optional)

Warmed caramel, for serving (optional)

1. Preheat oven to 350°F. Line an 8×8-inch pan with parchment paper and grease with cooking spray.

2. In a small saucepan over medium heat, melt butter. Cook, swirling pan occasionally, until deep golden bits collect on bottom of pan and butter smells nutty. Remove from heat immediately and let cool slightly.

3. In a large bowl, whisk together browned butter and sugars. Stir in egg, vanilla, and salt, then add flour, stirring until just combined. Fold in white chocolate chips and walnuts.

4. Press batter into prepared pan and smooth top. Bake until golden around edges and a toothpick inserted until center comes out with a few moist crumbs attached, 20 to 25 minutes. Let cool completely before slicing into squares and serving with ice cream and caramel, if desired.

BLONDIE MOMENTS
Play around with these fun variations.

CHIPS
- Butterscotch
- Peanut butter
- Dark chocolate

NUTS
- Pecans
- Roasted peanuts
- Pistachios

COWBOY BLONDIES

TOTAL TIME: 45 MIN / MAKES 15

A riff on Texas cowboy cookies—a cult treat in the Lone Star state—these blondies are loaded with pretty much everything in your pantry: chocolate and peanut butter chips, oats, coconut, and pecans. A little cinnamon makes the batter totally addictive.

Cooking spray

2 cups all-purpose flour

1 teaspoon ground cinnamon

1 teaspoon baking soda

½ teaspoon kosher salt

¾ cup (1½ sticks) butter, softened

1¼ cups granulated sugar

2 large eggs

2 teaspoons pure vanilla extract

1 cup semisweet chocolate chips

½ cup peanut butter chips

½ cup old-fashioned rolled oats

½ cup sweetened shredded coconut

⅓ cup finely chopped pecans

Warmed caramel, for drizzling

1. Preheat oven to 350°F. Line a 9×13-inch pan with parchment paper and grease with cooking spray.

2. In a medium bowl, whisk together flour, cinnamon, baking soda, and salt.

3. In a large bowl using a hand mixer, beat butter and sugar until light and fluffy. Add eggs, one at a time, and beat until incorporated, then add vanilla. Add dry ingredients to wet ingredients and beat until just combined. Fold in chocolate chips, peanut butter chips, oats, coconut, and pecans.

4. Press batter into prepared pan. (It will be thick.) Bake until golden, 20 to 22 minutes. Let cool completely.

5. Drizzle with caramel before slicing into squares and serving.

BIRTHDAY CAKE BLONDIES

TOTAL TIME: 1 HR 15 MIN / MAKES 20

If you fall into the camp who believes sprinkles make everything better, these are the only blondies you'll ever need to bake. Don't love white chocolate? Opt for semisweet chips.

Cooking spray

3 cups all-purpose flour

1½ teaspoons kosher salt

1 teaspoon baking powder

1 cup (2 sticks) plus 2 tablespoons butter, softened

1½ cups granulated sugar

¾ cup packed brown sugar

3 large eggs

1 tablespoon pure vanilla extract

2¼ cups white chocolate chips, divided

1 cup rainbow sprinkles, divided

1. Preheat oven to 350°F. Line a 9×13-inch pan with parchment paper and grease with cooking spray.

2. In a medium bowl, whisk together flour, salt, and baking powder.

3. In a large bowl using a hand mixer, beat butter and sugars until fluffy. Add eggs, one at a time, and beat until incorporated, then add vanilla. Add dry ingredients to wet ingredients and beat until just combined. Fold in 1½ cups of white chocolate chips and ¾ cup of sprinkles.

4. Press batter into prepared pan and sprinkle with ¼ cup of white chocolate chips and remaining ¼ cup sprinkles. Bake until edges are golden, about 30 minutes. Let cool completely.

5. Melt remaining ½ cup white chocolate chips in microwave until smooth, then drizzle over blondies before slicing into squares and serving.

COOKIES 'N' CREAM BLONDIES

TOTAL TIME: 50 MIN / MAKES 15

When blondies have Cookies 'n' Creme bars and Oreos in their batter, they have SO much more fun. This is the blondie recipe that made us fall in love with blondies. Bookmark these as the treat everyone deserves on their birthday.

Cooking spray

2¼ cups all-purpose flour

1 teaspoon kosher salt

½ teaspoon baking soda

¾ cup (1½ sticks) melted butter

1 cup granulated sugar

½ cup packed brown sugar

2 large eggs

1 teaspoon pure vanilla extract

1½ cups chopped Hershey's Cookies 'n' Creme bars, divided

1½ cups chopped Oreos (about 15), divided

1. Preheat oven to 350°F. Line a 9×13-inch pan with parchment paper and grease with cooking spray.

2. In a medium bowl, whisk together flour, salt, and baking soda.

3. In a large bowl using a hand mixer, beat melted butter and sugars until combined. Add eggs, one at a time, and beat until incorporated, then add vanilla. Gradually add dry ingredients to wet ingredients and beat until just combined. Fold in 1 cup each of chopped Cookies 'n' Creme bars and Oreos.

4. Press batter into prepared pan and top with remaining ½ cup each chopped Cookies 'n' Creme bars and Oreos.

5. Bake until edges are just golden, about 22 minutes. Let blondies cool completely before slicing into squares and serving.

LOADED PEANUT BUTTER BLONDIES

TOTAL TIME: 45 MIN / MAKES 24

Honestly, true peanut butter lovers might not even be able to handle these babies. There's peanut butter in the batter, they're stuffed with mini Reese's, and they get drizzled with even more peanut butter once they're baked. Byyyeee.

Cooking spray

2 cups all-purpose flour

1 teaspoon baking powder

1 teaspoon kosher salt

¾ cup (1½ sticks) butter, softened

1 cup peanut butter, divided

1 cup granulated sugar

½ cup packed brown sugar

2 large eggs

2 teaspoons pure vanilla extract

30 Reese's Miniatures, unwrapped

1 cup semisweet chocolate chips, melted

1. Preheat oven to 350°F. Line a 9×13-inch pan with parchment paper and grease with cooking spray.

2. In a medium bowl, whisk together flour, baking powder, and salt.

3. In a large bowl using a hand mixer, beat butter, ½ cup of peanut butter, and sugars until fluffy. Add eggs, one at a time, and beat until incorporated, then add vanilla. Add dry ingredients to wet ingredients and mix until just combined.

4. Press batter into prepared pan. Press Reese's candies into batter, creating even rows. Bake until blondies are just set, 25 to 30 minutes. Let cool completely.

5. Melt remaining ½ cup peanut butter in the microwave. Drizzle blondies with melted chocolate and peanut butter before slicing into squares and serving.

We like pushing the **REESE'S CANDIES** in on their sides (so that the ridges are facing up) for no reason other than the baked results looks 'grammable AF.

FLUFFERNUTTER BLONDIES

TOTAL TIME: 50 MIN / MAKES 9

If you grew up knowing anything, it was that a PB&J had absolutely nothing on a peanut butter–marshmallow Fluff sandwich. These blondies let you revisit the addictive, sweet combo as an adult.

Cooking spray

1¼ cups all-purpose flour

1 teaspoon baking powder

½ teaspoon kosher salt

½ cup (1 stick) melted butter

2 large eggs

1 cup packed brown sugar

½ cup granulated sugar

1 cup smooth peanut butter, divided

¼ cup marshmallow creme

1. Preheat oven to 350°F. Line a 9×9-inch pan with parchment paper and grease with cooking spray.

2. In a medium bowl, whisk together flour, baking powder, and salt.

3. In a large bowl, stir together melted butter, eggs, sugars, and ¾ cup of peanut butter. Gradually fold dry ingredients into wet ingredients until combined.

4. Microwave remaining ¼ cup peanut butter on low for 15 seconds. Press batter into prepared pan and drizzle batter with melted peanut butter. Microwave marshmallow creme on low for 15 seconds. Dollop with marshmallow creme, then swirl gently with a spoon.

5. Bake until golden and set, about 35 minutes. Let cool completely before slicing and serving.

ROLO-STUFFED BLONDIES

TOTAL TIME: 45 MIN / MAKES 12

You could stuff just about any type of chocolate bar into blondies (think Snickers, Twix, or Butterfinger), but this is our love letter to the Rolo, the most underrated candy, IOHO. With each bite of blondie, you get melty milk chocolate and oozing caramel.

Cooking spray

2 cups all-purpose flour

1 teaspoon baking soda

½ teaspoon kosher salt

¾ cup (1½ sticks) butter, softened

1¼ cups granulated sugar

2 large eggs

2 teaspoons pure vanilla extract

20 Rolos, unwrapped

½ cup caramel

½ cup semisweet chocolate chips, melted

1. Preheat oven to 350°F. Line an 8×8-inch pan with parchment paper and grease with cooking spray.

2. In a medium bowl, whisk together flour, baking soda, and salt.

3. In a large bowl using a hand mixer, beat butter and sugar until fluffy. Add eggs, one at a time, and beat until incorporated, then add vanilla. Add dry ingredients to wet ingredients and beat until just combined.

4. Press batter into prepared pan. Press Rolos slightly into batter, spacing them ½ inch apart. Bake until golden, 27 to 30 minutes. Let cool completely.

5. Drizzle blondies with caramel and melted chocolate before slicing into squares and serving.

CHAPTER FIVE

RAISING THE BAR

RAINBOW
CHEESECAKE
BARS, PG 167!

SLUTTY CHEESECAKE BARS

TOTAL TIME: 3 HR 55 MIN (INCLUDES CHILLING) / MAKES 9

The day we made these, we had "feelings" that they'd get around the internet (wink), which is exactly what happened. Because LOOK. AT. THEM. Cheesecake, chocolate chip cookie dough, Oreos, and warm caramel all stack up into one big cheat-day goal.

1 (16.5-ounce) log refrigerated chocolate chip cookie dough

20 Oreos, plus more for topping

2 (8-ounce) blocks cream cheese, softened

½ cup granulated sugar

2 large eggs

½ teaspoon pure vanilla extract

Pinch kosher salt

Warm caramel, for drizzling

1. Preheat oven to 325°F. Line an 8×8-inch pan with parchment paper, leaving a 2-inch overhang on two sides.

2. Press cookie dough into bottom of prepared pan and top with a single layer of Oreos, breaking them up to fit, if necessary.

3. In a large bowl using a hand mixer, beat cream cheese until smooth. Add sugar, eggs, vanilla, and salt and beat until incorporated.

4. Pour cream cheese mixture over Oreo layer and smooth top. Top with broken Oreo pieces and bake until center is only slightly jiggly, 30 to 35 minutes. Let cool to room temperature.

5. Refrigerate until completely chilled, at least 3 hours and up to overnight.

6. Drizzle with caramel before slicing into squares and serving.

Love margaritas? You can turn these into **BOOZY BARS** by swapping out the lemons for limes and spiking the filling with 3 tablespoons tequila.

INSANE LEMON BARS

Two things to look for when matching with your dream lemon bar (spoiler: this is it): an ultra-buttery crust and punchy sweet-tart flavor. Serve these at brunch or a bridal shower, and we guarantee everyone will ask for the recipe.

FOR THE CRUST

Cooking spray

1 cup (2 sticks) butter, cubed and softened

¾ cup granulated sugar

2½ cups all-purpose flour

¼ cup powdered sugar, plus more for dusting

FOR THE FILLING

2 cups granulated sugar

¼ cup all-purpose flour

6 large eggs

Zest of 1 lemon

¾ cup fresh lemon juice (about 4 lemons)

Small lemon wedges, for garnish

1. Make crust: Preheat oven to 350°F. Line a 9×13-inch pan with parchment paper and grease with cooking spray.

2. In a large bowl using a hand mixer, beat butter and granulated sugar until fluffy. Add flour and powdered sugar and beat until combined.

3. Press dough into prepared pan and bake until lightly golden, 18 to 20 minutes. Let cool 30 minutes. Keep oven on.

4. Make filling: In a large bowl, whisk together sugar, flour, eggs, lemon zest, and lemon juice. Pour filling over crust, return to oven, and bake until firm, about 20 minutes. Let cool to room temperature.

5. Refrigerate until chilled, 3 to 4 hours. Dust with powdered sugar, and garnish with lemon wedges.

OATMEAL FUDGE BARS

TOTAL TIME: 1 HR / MAKES 12

Imagine this: Buttery oatmeal cookies sandwiching the creamiest, dreamiest, most chocolatey fudge ever. It's so amazing, we made the fudge layer just as thick as the cookie.

FOR THE FILLING

1 (14-ounce) can sweetened condensed milk

1 (12-ounce) bag semisweet chocolate chips

2 tablespoons butter

¼ teaspoon kosher salt

FOR COOKIE LAYERS

Cooking spray

2 cups all-purpose flour

2 cups quick-cooking oats

1 teaspoon baking powder

1 teaspoon kosher salt

1 cup (2 sticks) butter, softened

¾ cup lightly packed brown sugar

¾ cup granulated sugar

1 teaspoon pure vanilla extract

2 large eggs

1. Preheat oven to 350°F. Line a 9×13-inch pan with parchment paper and grease with cooking spray.

2. Make filling: In a medium saucepan over medium-low heat, heat condensed milk, chocolate chips, butter, and salt, stirring often, until melted. Remove from heat.

3. Make cookie layers: In a medium bowl, whisk together flour, oats, baking powder, and salt.

4. In a large bowl using a hand mixer, beat butter, sugars, and vanilla until light and fluffy. Add eggs, one at a time, and beat until incorporated, then add dry ingredients and mix until just combined.

5. Spread about half the cookie dough into prepared pan in an even layer, then spread filling over the top. Top with remaining cookie dough.

6. Bake until set and lightly golden on top, 40 minutes. Let cool to room temperature before slicing and serving.

 If you end up using too much **COOKIE DOUGH** on the bottom and can't make an even top layer, it's okay to just scatter the remaining dough over the top in big clumps; they'll spread as the bars bake.

CARAMEL APPLE BARS

TOTAL TIME: 1 HR / MAKES 20

When you want to make enough apple pie for everybody, don't hunker down and bake three apple pies—make these instead. The press-in crust is no fuss (zero rolling required!) and the crumb topping is majorly addicting.

FOR THE CRUST

Cooking spray

1 cup (2 sticks) butter, softened

½ cup granulated sugar

¼ cup packed brown sugar

2½ cups all-purpose flour

½ teaspoon kosher salt

FOR THE FILLING

6 apples, peeled, cored, and sliced

Juice of ½ lemon

½ cup lightly packed brown sugar

1 teaspoon ground cinnamon

1 teaspoon pure vanilla extract

½ teaspoon kosher salt

FOR THE TOPPING

1½ cups all-purpose flour

1 cup chopped pecans

1 cup packed brown sugar

½ teaspoon kosher salt

¾ cup (1½ sticks) melted butter

Caramel, for serving

1. Make crust: Preheat oven to 350°F and grease a 9×13-inch pan with cooking spray.

2. In a large bowl using a hand mixer, beat butter and sugars until light and fluffy. Add flour and salt and mix until just combined. Press into prepared pan. Bake until lightly golden, 20 minutes.

3. Make filling: In a large bowl, toss apples, lemon juice, brown sugar, cinnamon, vanilla, and salt. Spread apples over crust.

4. Make topping: In a medium bowl, whisk together flour, pecans, brown sugar, and salt. Stir in melted butter until texture is coarse and sandy. Sprinkle crumb topping over apples.

5. Bake until top is golden and apples are soft, about 30 minutes. Let cool 15 minutes, then slice into squares and drizzle with caramel before serving.

SNICKERDOODLE CHEESECAKE BARS

TOTAL TIME: 1 HR 30 MIN / MAKES 24

One of our most popular desserts of all time because the only way to make a snickerdoodle blondie better is to layer it with cheesecake. Don't worry if the top of the cheesecake isn't perfectly covered with cookie dough; it's meant to look a little craggly.

FOR THE SNICKER-DOODLE LAYER

2¼ cups all-purpose flour

½ teaspoon baking soda

1½ teaspoons ground cinnamon

1 teaspoon kosher salt

¾ cup (1½ sticks) melted butter

1 cup granulated sugar

½ cup packed brown sugar

2 large eggs

1 teaspoon pure vanilla extract

¼ cup cinnamon-sugar

FOR THE CHEESECAKE LAYER

Cooking spray

2 (8-ounce) blocks cream cheese, softened

½ cup granulated sugar

2 large eggs

½ teaspoon pure vanilla extract

Pinch kosher salt

1. Preheat oven to 350°F and grease a 9×13-inch pan with cooking spray.

2. Make snickerdoodle layer: In a medium bowl, whisk together flour, baking soda, cinnamon, and salt.

3. In a large bowl using a hand mixer, beat melted butter and sugars until incorporated. Add eggs, one at a time, and beat until incorporated, then add vanilla. Gradually add dry ingredients to wet ingredients and mix until just combined.

4. Make cheesecake layer: In a large bowl using a hand mixer, beat cream cheese and granulated sugar until fluffy. Add eggs, one at a time, and beat until incorporated, then add vanilla and salt.

5. Press about half the snickerdoodle dough into prepared pan and sprinkle with half the cinnamon-sugar. Pour cheesecake batter on top and smooth with a rubber spatula. Break up remaining snickerdoodle dough into small clumps, flatten slightly with your hands, and dot all over cheesecake layer. Sprinkle with remaining cinnamon-sugar.

6. Bake until edges are set and center of cheesecake is only slightly jiggly, about 40 minutes. Let cool completely before slicing into squares and serving.

MILLIONAIRE SHORTBREAD

TOTAL TIME: 1 HR 45 MIN / MAKES 24

This spectacle of a dessert has three layers—shortbread crust, chewy caramel, and chocolate—finished with a little salt because that's how we roll. It's basically a homemade Twix bar, only a millionaire times better.

FOR THE SHORTBREAD LAYER

Cooking spray

1 cup (2 sticks) butter, softened

¾ cup granulated sugar

2¼ cups all-purpose flour

1 teaspoon pure vanilla extract

1 teaspoon kosher salt

FOR THE CARAMEL LAYER

2 (11-ounce) packages caramel squares

½ cup heavy cream

FOR THE CHOCOLATE LAYER

2 cups semisweet chocolate chips, melted

Flaky sea salt

1. Make shortbread layer: Preheat oven to 300°F. Line a 9×13-inch pan with parchment paper and grease with cooking spray.

2. In a large bowl using a hand mixer, beat butter and sugar until light and fluffy. Add flour, vanilla, and salt and mix until a breadcrumb texture forms.

3. Press mixture into prepared pan and prick all over with a fork. Bake until lightly golden, about 35 minutes. Let cool completely.

4. Make caramel layer: In a small saucepan over medium-low heat, heat caramels and heavy cream, stirring constantly, until melted, about 5 minutes. Pour over cooled shortbread layer.

5. Pour melted chocolate over caramel layer and smooth top with a spatula. Refrigerate until firm, 20 minutes, then sprinkle with flaky salt before slicing into bars and serving.

RAINBOW CHEESECAKE BARS

TOTAL TIME: 4 HR (INCLUDING CHILLING) / MAKES 20

Can't stop staring? We know the feeling. The mesmerizing, vibrant swirls on these colorful bars will make all your friends pull out their phones to Instagram them before digging in.

FOR THE CRUST

Cooking spray

18 graham crackers, crushed

¾ cup (1½ sticks) melted butter

½ cup granulated sugar

FOR THE FILLING

4 (8-ounce) blocks cream cheese, softened

½ cup sour cream

1⅓ cups granulated sugar

6 large eggs

2 teaspoons pure vanilla extract

1 teaspoon kosher salt

Neon food coloring in 6 colors

1. Make crust: Preheat oven to 325°F and grease an 9×13-inch pan with cooking spray.

2. In a medium bowl, stir together crushed graham crackers, melted butter, and sugar until combined. Press into prepared pan.

3. Make filling: In a large bowl using a hand mixer, beat cream cheese, sour cream, and sugar until smooth. Add eggs, vanilla, and salt and beat until incorporated. Pour about half the cheesecake mixture into pan.

4. Divide remaining cheesecake mixture among six small bowls (one bowl for each color you're using) and add a couple drops of food coloring to each bowl. Stir to combine, adjusting colors as desired.

5. Add spoonfuls of the dyed cheesecake mixture to the plain cheesecake mixture, alternating colors until you've used up the whole mixture. Using a butter knife, swirl colors together.

6. Place pan inside a large roasting pan and pour in enough boiling water to come halfway up the sides. Bake until only slightly jiggly, about 45 minutes. Turn off oven and prop open oven door slightly. Let cool in oven 1 hour. Remove pan from water and cover with plastic wrap. Refrigerate until firm, at least 3 hours or up to overnight. Slice into bars and serve.

SAMOA CHEESECAKE BARS

TOTAL TIME: 3 HR 50 MIN (INCLUDING CHILLING) / MAKES 12

Every year around Girl Scout cookie season, the Delish office hoards as many boxes of Samoas as possible—for "research." We love giving our favorite desserts (brownies, pie, truffles) the Samoa treatment by slathering them with this irresistible coconutty, caramelly topping.

FOR THE CRUST

28 Oreos, finely crushed

5 tablespoons melted butter

FOR THE CHEESECAKE

2 (8-ounce) blocks cream cheese, softened

½ cup granulated sugar

2 large eggs

½ teaspoon pure vanilla extract

Pinch kosher salt

FOR THE TOPPING

1½ cups caramel, divided

1½ cups sweetened shredded coconut, toasted

Melted chocolate, for drizzling

1. Preheat oven to 325°F and line a 9×13-inch pan with foil, leaving a 2-inch overhang on two sides.

2. Make crust: In a large bowl, stir together crushed Oreos and melted butter until combined. Pat mixture into prepared pan.

3. Make cheesecake layer: In a large bowl using a hand mixer, beat cream cheese and sugar until smooth. Add eggs, vanilla, and salt and beat until incorporated.

4. Pour cheesecake mixture over crust and bake until only slightly jiggly, about 35 minutes. Let cool slightly, then cover with plastic wrap and refrigerate until completely chilled, at least 3 hours and preferably overnight.

5. When ready to serve, pour 1 cup of caramel over cheesecake bars and smooth with a spatula.

6. In a small bowl, stir together toasted coconut and remaining ½ cup caramel. Sprinkle over bars and drizzle with melted chocolate. Refrigerate 10 minutes before slicing into squares and serving.

OREOGASM RICE KRISPIE

TOTAL TIME: 30 MIN / MAKES 16

We know what you're thinking: Aren't classic Rice Krispies treats perfect as is?! Yes, sure, but stuffing them with a layer of whole Oreos and stirring crushed Oreos into the mixture just proves what monsters we really are.

Cooking spray

5 tablespoons butter

1 (10-ounce) bag mini marshmallows

Pinch kosher salt

6 cups Rice Krispies

36 Oreos: 24 kept whole, 12 crushed, divided

⅓ cup white chocolate chips

1 teaspoon coconut oil, divided

⅓ cup semisweet chocolate chips

1. Line a 9×13-inch pan with parchment paper and grease with cooking spray.

2. In a large pot over medium-low heat, melt butter. Add marshmallows and salt and stir until mixture is melted.

3. Remove from heat, then immediately add Rice Krispies and half the crushed Oreos and stir until combined.

4. Working quickly, press half the mixture into an even layer in prepared pan, then top with a layer of whole Oreos. Press remaining Rice Krispies mixture over whole Oreos and top with remaining crushed Oreos.

5. In a small microwave-safe bowl, melt white chocolate chips and ½ teaspoon of coconut oil until smooth. In a separate bowl, melt semisweet chocolate chips and remaining ½ teaspoon coconut oil until smooth.

6. Drizzle Krispie treats with both chocolates and let set 15 minutes before slicing into squares and serving.

PEANUT BUTTER-IFY these by swapping out the Oreos for Reese's cups and stirring ½ cup creamy peanut butter into the Rice Krispie mixture.

BANANA PUDDING BARS

TOTAL TIME: 6 HR 20 MIN (INCLUDING CHILLING) / MAKES 20

The classic banana pudding reincarnated as a classy bake sale dessert. The no-bake cheesecake-like filling of vanilla pudding, cream cheese, and Cool Whip will haunt your dreams.

FOR CRUST

3 cups crushed Nilla wafers

½ cup (1 stick) melted butter

¼ cup sugar

¼ teaspoon kosher salt

FOR FILLING

3 (8-ounce) blocks cream cheese, softened

1 cup granulated sugar

2 cups Cool Whip

1 (5.1-ounce) package instant banana pudding mix

3 cups whole milk

FOR TOPPING

Cool Whip

1 banana, sliced

20 Nilla wafers

1. Line an 9×13-inch pan with parchment paper.

2. Make crust: In a medium bowl, stir together Nilla wafers, melted butter, sugar, and salt. Press into prepared pan. Transfer to freezer while you make filling.

3. Make cheesecake filling: In a large bowl using a hand mixer, beat cream cheese until fluffy. Add sugar and beat until combined, then fold in Cool Whip.

4. In a medium bowl, whisk together pudding mix and milk. Transfer pudding to refrigerator and let stand 3 minutes, until thickened. Fold pudding into cheesecake mixture until incorporated and no streaks remain.

5. Pour filling over prepared crust and smooth into an even layer. Cover with plastic wrap and freeze until bars are firm, at least 6 hours and up to overnight.

6. When ready to serve, remove from freezer and slice into squares. Top each square with a dollop of Cool Whip, a slice of banana, and a Nilla wafer.

S'MORES SKILLET COOKIE, PG 179!

CHAPTER SIX

GIANT BITES

DEATH BY CHOCOLATE SKILLET BROWNIE

TOTAL TIME: 45 MIN / SERVES 8

This brownie is like a religion at Delish. The chocolate chip trifecta—milk, white, and dark all go into the batter—is what makes staffers turn to it again and again to get through a sh*tty week.

Cooking spray

2¾ cups dark chocolate chips, divided

¾ cup (1 stick) butter, softened

¾ cup granulated sugar

¾ cup packed brown sugar

3 large eggs

1 tablespoon pure vanilla extract

1 cup all-purpose flour

3 tablespoons unsweetened cocoa powder

¾ teaspoon kosher salt

¾ cup milk chocolate chips

¾ cup white chocolate chips

Ice cream, for serving

Warm hot fudge, for serving

1. Preheat oven to 350°F and grease a 10-inch ovenproof skillet with cooking spray.

2. In a heatproof medium bowl, microwave 2 cups of dark chocolate chips and butter until melted. Stir until smooth, then add sugars and whisk until incorporated. Add eggs and vanilla and stir until incorporated.

3. In a separate bowl, combine the flour, cocoa powder, and salt, then fold dry ingredients into wet ingredients until just a bit of flour mixture remains visible. Gently fold in all chocolate chips, including the remaining ¾ cup dark chocolate chips.

4. Transfer batter to prepared skillet. Bake until a toothpick inserted into center comes out with a few moist crumbs attached, about 30 minutes. Serve warm with ice cream and hot fudge.

Don't have an **OVENPROOF SKILLET**? You can make any of our skillet cookies in a 9-inch round cake pan instead.

S'MORES SKILLET COOKIE

TOTAL TIME: 45 MIN / SERVES 12

Crushed graham crackers make the dough impossible to stop eating, and the ring of melty marshmallows makes it impossible to stop staring.

Cooking spray

1½ cups all-purpose flour

¼ cup crushed graham crackers

½ teaspoon baking soda

¼ teaspoon kosher salt

¾ cup (1½ sticks) butter, softened

½ cup packed brown sugar

⅓ cup granulated sugar

2 large eggs

1½ teaspoons pure vanilla extract

1 cup semisweet chocolate chips

3 Hershey's bars, broken into smaller pieces, divided

1 cup mini marshmallows, divided

11 marshmallows, halved

1. Preheat oven to 350°F and grease a 10-inch ovenproof skillet with cooking spray.

2. In a medium bowl, whisk together flour, crushed graham crackers, baking soda, and salt.

3. In a large bowl using a hand mixer, beat butter and sugars until light and fluffy. Add eggs and vanilla and beat until incorporated. Add dry ingredients and mix until just combined, then fold in chocolate chips and most of the Hershey's bars and mini marshmallows.

4. Press dough into prepared skillet and top with remaining Hershey's bars and mini marshmallows. Bake until center is almost set, 22 to 25 minutes.

5. Place marshmallows cut-side down around outside edge of cookie. Return to oven and bake until puffed and golden, 5 to 8 minutes more.

GIANT OREO CAKE

TOTAL TIME: 45 MIN / SERVES 12

The Oreo lover inside of you (it's there—don't even try to pretend) will freak over this larger-than-life cake. The sugary filling tastes eerily similar to the real thing. Best served with a cold glass of milk.

FOR THE COOKIES

Cooking spray

2½ cups all-purpose flour

2 cups granulated sugar

1 cup packed brown sugar

1 cup unsweetened dark cocoa powder

2 teaspoons baking soda

½ teaspoon baking powder

½ teaspoon kosher salt

1 cup (2 sticks) butter, softened

2 large eggs

FOR THE FILLING

1 cup (2 sticks) butter, softened

2 teaspoons pure vanilla extract

4 cups powdered sugar

1. Make cookies: Preheat oven to 350°F. Line two 8-inch round cake pans with parchment paper and grease with cooking spray.

2. In a large bowl, whisk together flour, sugars, cocoa powder, baking soda, baking powder, and salt. Add butter and, using a hand mixer, mix on low speed until dough starts to come together in a mass. Add eggs and mix until incorporated. (The dough should feel sandy.)

3. Press dough into prepared pans, then press a large fork around the edges of the cookie to make indentations similar to those on an Oreo. Bake until cookies are slightly crackly on top, about 20 minutes. Let cool in pans 10 minutes, then invert onto wire racks to cool completely.

4. Make filling: In a large bowl using a hand mixer, beat butter and vanilla until smooth and fluffy. Gradually add powdered sugar, about 1 cup at a time, and beat until smooth.

5. Gather filling into a large ball and transfer to a piece of parchment paper. Pat filling into a large disc, about 8 inches in diameter.

6. Transfer one cooled cookie to a serving dish. (Save the prettier of the two for the top.) Place filling on top, then sandwich with remaining cookie, indentation-side up. Slice into wedges before serving.

CHOCOLATE CHIP SKILLET COOKIE

TOTAL TIME: 40 MIN / SERVES 12

Some people think sharing circles and trust falls are the ultimate bonding moments. For us, nothing beats elbowing each other out of the way for another bite of cookie. Top this with ice cream, caramel, and chocolate sauce; gather your favorite people; and stuff your face.

Cooking spray

½ cup (1 stick) butter, softened

½ cup granulated sugar

¾ cup packed light brown sugar

1 large egg

1 teaspoon pure vanilla extract

1¾ cups all-purpose flour

¾ teaspoon baking soda

½ teaspoon kosher salt

1¼ cups semisweet chocolate chips, divided

Pinch flaky sea salt

FOR SERVING

Vanilla ice cream

Caramel sauce, warmed

Chocolate syrup

1. Preheat oven to 350°F and grease a 10-inch ovenproof skillet with cooking spray.

2. In a large bowl using a hand mixer, beat butter and sugars until light and fluffy. Add egg and vanilla and beat until incorporated. Add flour, baking soda, and salt and mix until just combined. Fold in 1 cup of chocolate chips.

3. Press dough into prepared skillet and top with remaining ¼ cup chocolate chips. Sprinkle with flaky salt. Bake until edges are golden, 20 to 24 minutes.

4. Serve warm with ice cream, caramel, and chocolate syrup.

DŌ COOKIE DOUGH CONFECTIONS
NEW YORK

NYC'S DŌ is proof dreams really do come true—or, rather, *dough* come true, as the neon sign at the café's entrance reads. The spot is a veritable shrine to cookie dough: It's served by the scoop like ice cream, stuffed into fudge squares and pie slices, and baked into what founder and CEO Kristen Tomlan calls "confections"— cookie-forward riffs on classic bakery treats like brownies and cake.

The Cookie Bomb is DŌ's answer to a traditional cupcake: a stuffed cookie cup with cookie dough frosting and a ball of straight-up cookie dough on top—like a cherry, only better. "It didn't make sense for us to go the traditional route and just do cookie dough in the frosting," Kristen says. The Cookie Bomb debuted on the café's inaugural menu; it hasn't gone anywhere since. "We still carry the two flavors we launched with, Nutella-stuffed and sprinkle-stuffed, but we've done *so* many other versions," Kristen recalls. "We've dyed the frosting, added Fruity Pebbles, changed the flavor of cookie dough." For Delish, Kristen dreamed up an entirely new twist on the Cookie Bomb, one made with cake batter dough (one of the shop's most popular flavors, second only to classic), stuffed with sprinkles, and topped with cake batter frosting. To her, it's the best of both worlds: "You get the sense you're eating a cupcake from the cake batter flavor, but you get the most fudgy, chewy cookie at the bottom."

DŌ COOKIE DOUGH CONFECTIONS'
FUNFETTI COOKIE BOMB

TOTAL TIME: 3 HR / MAKES 12

FOR THE COOKIE DOUGH

1½ cups all-purpose flour

1½ cups Funfetti cake mix (about ½ box)

1 tablespoon cornstarch

½ teaspoon salt

¾ cup (1½ sticks) butter, softened

½ cup granulated sugar

½ cup packed brown sugar

1 large egg

2 teaspoons clear imitation vanilla extract

½ cup plus ⅓ cup sprinkles

½ cup mini semisweet chocolate chips

FOR THE FROSTING AND TOPPING

1 cup (2 sticks) butter, softened

1 tablespoon clear imitation vanilla extract

1 tablespoon heavy cream

1 teaspoon kosher salt

3 cups powdered sugar, sifted

⅔ cup sprinkles, divided

⅓ cup sprinkles

1. Make cookie dough: In a medium bowl, whisk together flour, cake mix, cornstarch, and salt.

2. In the bowl of a stand mixer fitted with the paddle attachment, beat butter until smooth and creamy. Add sugars and mix until light and fluffy. Add egg and vanilla and mix until fully incorporated, about 2 minutes.

3. Add half the dry ingredients and beat just until the powdery texture of the mixture disappears, about 15 seconds. Add remaining flour mixture and beat until combined. Fold in ½ cup of sprinkles and chocolate chips.

RECIPE CONTINUES

4. Refrigerate dough for 1 hour. Once chilled, divide dough into 13 even portions and roll into balls. Freeze for 30 minutes.

5. Meanwhile, preheat oven to 350°F and line a muffin tin with cupcake liners.

6. Remove 12 dough balls from freezer and use your thumbs to press into center of each ball, forming a bowl shape in the palm of your hand. Fill each hole with 1 teaspoon of remaining sprinkles, then use your fingers to pinch the cookie dough over the sprinkles. Roll ball until sprinkles are completely concealed. Place stuffed ball into cupcake liner. Repeat with 11 more balls and sprinkles.

7. Bake until edges are golden, 15 to 20 minutes. Let cool in pan for about 5 minutes, then transfer to a wire rack to cool completely.

8. Meanwhile, make frosting: In the bowl of a stand mixer fitted with the paddle attachment, beat butter speed until light and fluffy. Add vanilla, heavy cream, and salt and mix until combined.

9. Add powdered sugar ½ cup at a time until incorporated. Then turn the mixer to high and beat until frosting is super light and fluffy, at least 5 minutes. With the mixer running, add sprinkles 2 tablespoons at a time until combined. Transfer frosting to a piping bag.

10. Pipe frosting onto each cookie bomb and place on top of cupcakes. Garnish with remaining sprinkles. Pull off small chunks of remaining cookie dough ball and roll into balls, then place one on top of each bomb before serving. Store cookie bombs in an airtight container in refrigerator up to 3 days.

SLOW-COOKER BROWNIE

TOTAL TIME: 5 HR 10 MIN / SERVES 8

Just when we think we've exhausted our slow cooker's endless talents, we try something crazy like brownies—and it totally works. The slow-cooking process makes the texture dangerously fudgy. Best served family-style, with a stack of spoons.

Cooking spray

1 cup (2 sticks) melted butter

1¼ cups granulated sugar

¼ cup packed brown sugar

⅔ cup unsweetened cocoa powder

⅓ cup all-purpose flour

3 large eggs

1 teaspoon pure vanilla extract

½ teaspoon kosher salt

1 cup semisweet chocolate chips

Ice cream, for serving

Whipped cream, for serving

Rainbow sprinkles, for serving

Maraschino cherries, for serving

1. Grease the bowl of your slow cooker with cooking spray.

2. In a large bowl, whisk together melted butter, sugars, cocoa powder, flour, eggs, vanilla, and salt until smooth. Fold in chocolate chips and pour batter into prepared slow cooker.

3. Cover and cook on low until brownie is set around the edges and slightly gooey in the center, about 5 hours.

4. Scoop brownies into bowls, then top each bowl with ice cream, whipped cream, sprinkles, and a cherry.

 This recipe works perfectly in a 4-quart **SLOW COOKER**. If yours is bigger (or smaller), you'll need to adjust your cook time.

GIANT COOKIE CAKE

TOTAL TIME: 25 MIN / SERVES 10

Who says a cookie doesn't count as a cake?! This is like one of those giant Mrs. Fields cookies you always stared at longingly while passing the booth in the mall—only so much better.

FOR THE COOKIE
Cooking spray

1 cup (2 sticks) butter, softened

¾ cup packed brown sugar

¾ cup granulated sugar

2 large eggs

2 teaspoons pure vanilla extract

2⅔ cups all-purpose flour

1 teaspoon baking soda

½ teaspoon kosher salt

2 cups semisweet chocolate chips, plus more for sprinkling

¼ cup rainbow sprinkles, plus more for sprinkling

FOR THE FROSTING
½ cup (1 stick) butter, softened

2 cups powdered sugar

1 tablespoon heavy cream

½ teaspoon pure vanilla extract

Pinch kosher salt

1. Make cookie: Preheat oven to 350°F. Line a 9-inch round cake pan with parchment paper and grease with cooking spray.

2. In a large bowl using a hand mixer, beat butter and sugars until light and fluffy. Add eggs, one at a time, and beat until incorporated, then add vanilla. Add flour, baking soda, and salt and beat on low until just combined. Fold in chocolate chips and rainbow sprinkles.

3. Press dough into prepared pan and top with more chocolate chips and sprinkles. Bake until golden, about 25 minutes. Let cool in pan 15 minutes, then transfer to a wire rack to cool completely.

4. Make frosting: In a large bowl using a hand mixer, beat butter until smooth. Add powdered sugar and beat until fluffy, then add heavy cream, vanilla, and salt and beat until smooth.

5. Transfer frosting to a piping bag fitted with a large star tip and frost edge of cooled cookie cake. Top with additional sprinkles and slice into wedges before serving.

 Pull the cookie from the oven **BEFORE YOU THINK IT'S READY.** If you poke it with a toothpick, it should come out with very moist crumbs attached.

GIANT OATMEAL CREME PIE

When Lauren had the idea to create a Little Debbie huge enough to be a birthday cake, we couldn't wait for the reveal. The oatmeal cookie is a little softer and the layer of frosting is much thicker than what you grew up with—discrepancies that upset absolutely no one.

FOR THE COOKIES

Cooking spray

1 cup (2 sticks) butter, softened

1 cup packed brown sugar

½ cup granulated sugar

2 large eggs

1 teaspoon pure vanilla extract

1¼ cups all-purpose flour

1¾ cups old-fashioned rolled oats

1 teaspoon baking powder

½ teaspoon ground cinnamon

½ teaspoon kosher salt

FOR THE FILLING

1 cup plus 2 tablespoons (2¼ sticks) butter, softened

2 cups powdered sugar

1 teaspoon pure vanilla extract

2 tablespoons milk

1. Make cookies: Preheat oven to 350°F. Grease two 8-inch cake pans with cooking spray and line bottoms with parchment paper.

2. In a large bowl using a hand mixer, beat butter and sugars until light and fluffy. Add eggs, one at a time, and beat until incorporated, then add vanilla. Add flour, oats, baking powder, cinnamon, and salt and beat until just combined.

3. Divide dough between prepared pans and press into an even layer. Bake until golden, about 25 minutes. Let cookies cool in pans 10 minutes, then invert onto wire racks and transfer to the fridge to cool completely, at least 30 minutes.

4. Meanwhile, make filling: In a large bowl using a hand mixer, beat butter, powdered sugar, and vanilla until smooth and fluffy. Add milk and beat until smooth.

5. Transfer one cooled cookie layer to a serving dish. Spread filling on top, then sandwich with second cookie. Slice into wedges before serving.

SLOW-COOKER CHOCOLATE CHIP COOKIE

TOTAL TIME: 3 HR 10 MIN / SERVES 8 TO 10

You can set and forget your slow cooker for like 6 hours, and it'll bake one mean cookie. It has something for every cookie preference: crisp and chewy around the edges, soft and melty in the middle. When you want a low-fi dessert for dinner guests, this is it.

½ cup (1 stick) butter, softened

½ cup granulated sugar

⅓ cup packed brown sugar

1 large egg

1 teaspoon pure vanilla extract

1½ cups all-purpose flour

1 teaspoon baking soda

Large pinch kosher salt

1½ cups semisweet chocolate chips

Chocolate syrup, for serving

1. Using two 4-inch strips of parchment paper, line the bowl of your slow cooker in an "X" formation. In a large bowl using a hand mixer, beat butter and sugars until light and fluffy. Add egg and vanilla and beat until incorporated, then add flour, baking soda, and salt and beat until fully combined. Fold in chocolate chips.

2. Transfer cookie dough to slow cooker and smooth top with a spatula. Cover and cook on low 5 to 6 hours or on high 2½ to 3 hours, until almost completely cooked through and only slightly soft in the center. (Cookie can be kept warm in slow cooker up to 3 hours.)

3. Remove bowl insert from slow cooker and transfer to a wire rack to cool. Using the parchment strips, lift cookie out of slow cooker, then slice and serve with chocolate syrup, if desired

CHRISTMAS LIGHT CUPCAKES, PG 224!

CHAPTER SEVEN

'TIS THE SEASON

PERFECT SUGAR COOKIES

TIME 1 HR 45 MIN / MAKES 24

Sugar cookies seem like the simplest cookie you can bake, but finding a trusty recipe can be surprisingly tough. Ours holds its shape, with sharp edges every time, which makes it ideal for cutting out and decorating. As for the frosting, a tiny splash of almond extract makes it unforgettable.

FOR THE COOKIES

3 cups all-purpose flour, plus more for dusting

1 teaspoon baking powder

½ teaspoon kosher salt

1 cup (2 sticks) butter, softened

1 cup granulated sugar

1 large egg

1 tablespoon milk

1 teaspoon pure vanilla extract

FOR THE FROSTING

1 cup (2 sticks) butter, softened

5 cups powdered sugar

¼ cup heavy cream

½ teaspoon pure almond extract

¼ teaspoon kosher salt

Food coloring

1. Make cookies: In a medium bowl, whisk together flour, baking powder, and salt.

2. In a large bowl using a hand mixer, beat butter and granulated sugar until light and fluffy. Add egg, milk, and vanilla and beat until combined. Gradually add dry ingredients to wet ingredients and beat until combined.

3. Shape dough into a disc and wrap with plastic wrap. Refrigerate until firm, about 1 hour.

4. When ready to roll, preheat oven to 350°F and line two large baking sheets with parchment paper.

5. Lightly flour a clean work surface and roll out dough to ⅛ inch thick. Cut out desired shapes and transfer to prepared baking sheets, spacing cookies 1 inch apart. Freeze cookies 10 minutes (so the shapes hold while baking), then bake until edges are lightly golden, 8 to 10 minutes. Let cool completely.

6. Make frosting: In a large bowl using a hand mixer, beat butter until smooth, then add powdered sugar and beat until no lumps remain. Add heavy cream, almond extract, and salt and beat until combined.

7. Frost and decorate cooled cookies as desired.

You can make this dough up to **3 DAYS** in advance. Wrap it in plastic wrap and store it in the fridge until you're ready to bake. Just be sure to bring to room temperature before rolling out.

SANTA'S TRASH COOKIES

TOTAL TIME: 1 HR / MAKES 20

Our most popular Christmas cookie of all time. Adding potato chips, pretzels, AND chocolate chips might sound insane (maybe even a little trashy), but people lose their minds over the super-salty, kinda sweet flavor.

2¼ cups all-purpose flour

½ teaspoon baking soda

½ teaspoon kosher salt

1 cup (2 sticks) butter, softened

½ cup granulated sugar

½ cup packed brown sugar

1 large egg

2 teaspoons pure vanilla extract

¾ cup crushed potato chips

¾ cup crushed pretzels

1¼ cups semisweet chocolate chips

½ cup red and green sprinkles

Flaky sea salt

1. Preheat oven to 350°F and line two large baking sheets with parchment paper.

2. In a medium bowl, whisk together flour, baking soda, and salt until combined.

3. In a large bowl using a hand mixer, beat butter and sugars until light and fluffy. Add egg and vanilla and beat until incorporated. Add dry ingredients to wet ingredients and mix until just combined.

4. Gently fold in most of the potato chips, pretzels, chocolate chips, and sprinkles (reserve some for pressing on tops of cookies).

5. Using a medium cookie scoop, scoop balls of dough (about 2 tablespoons each) onto prepared baking sheets, spacing cookies 2 inches apart. Press down lightly on each cookie to flatten, then press remaining potato chips, pretzels, chocolate chips, and sprinkles on top. Sprinkle with flaky salt.

6. Bake until edges are just starting to turn golden, about 14 minutes. Repeat with remaining ingredients.

We love the combo of **PUMPKIN** and **CHOCOLATE**, but you can also do a graham cracker or gingersnap crust. Sub in the same amount as the crushed Oreos.

PUMPKIN CRÈME BRÛLÉE CHEESECAKE BARS

TOTAL TIME: 4 HR (INCLUDES CHILLING) / MAKES 16

Pumpkin cheesecake on its own is one of our favorite holiday desserts. But with a thick, crackly layer of caramelized sugar on top? See you later.

FOR THE CRUST

Cooking spray

1½ cups finely crushed Oreos (about 15)

5 tablespoons melted butter

1 tablespoon granulated sugar

Pinch kosher salt

FOR THE FILLING

2 (8-ounce) blocks cream cheese, softened

1 cup pumpkin puree

½ cup plus 2 tablespoons granulated sugar, divided

¼ cup packed brown sugar

1 large egg

2 large egg yolks

1 teaspoon pure vanilla extract

1 teaspoon pumpkin pie spice

½ teaspoon kosher salt

1. Make crust: Preheat oven to 325°F and grease an 8×8-inch pan with cooking spray.

2. In a medium bowl, stir together crushed Oreos, melted butter, sugar, and salt. Press into prepared pan in an even layer.

3. Make filling: In a large bowl using a hand mixer, beat cream cheese, pumpkin, and sugars together until no lumps remain. Add egg and egg yolks, one at a time, and beat until incorporated, then stir in vanilla. Add pumpkin pie spice and salt and beat until just combined. Pour mixture over crust.

4. Place pan inside a large roasting pan and pour in enough boiling water to come halfway up the sides. Bake until only slightly jiggly, about 50 minutes. Turn off oven and prop open oven door slightly. Let cool in oven 1 hour. Remove pan from water and cover with plastic wrap. Refrigerate until firm, at least 2 hours or up to overnight.

5. When ready to serve, slice into bars. Sprinkle with an even layer of remaining 2 tablespoons sugar and, using a kitchen torch, caramelize sugar until golden.

LEG LAMP COOKIES

TOTAL TIME: 1 HR / MAKES 36

We knew these cookies were going to break the internet because
a) *A Christmas Story* is everyone's must-watch December movie,
and b) is there anything more iconic than the leg lamp?!

1 (16.5-ounce) log
refrigerated sugar
cookie dough

¼ cup all-purpose flour

1 (0.67-ounce) container
black cookie icing

9 (2.8-ounce) packages
Reese's Big Cups,
halved lengthwise

3 tablespoons creamy
peanut butter

¼ cup yellow icing

1. Preheat oven to 350°F and line two large baking
sheets with parchment paper.

2. In a large bowl, combine cookie dough and flour. On
a clean surface, roll out dough to ¼ inch thick. Freeze
20 minutes.

3. Using a paring knife, cut out cookies (use stencil on
page 206) **A**. Freeze dough 20 minutes more.

4. Transfer dough to prepared baking sheets, spacing
cookies 1 inch apart, and bake until lightly golden, 10 to
11 minutes. Let cool completely.

5. Using black cookie icing, draw a heel on each leg
lamp, as well as a crosshatch design to mimic fishnet
stockings **B C**. Refrigerate for 10 minutes to set icing.

6. Dab a little peanut butter on the cut side of each
Reese's, then press it on top of each cookie.

7. In a small bowl, stir together yellow icing and
2 teaspoons water. Coat Reese's with icing, filling in
crevices, to resemble a yellow lampshade **D**. Refrigerate
10 minutes to set icing before serving.

— WATCH & LEARN —

A   B   C   D

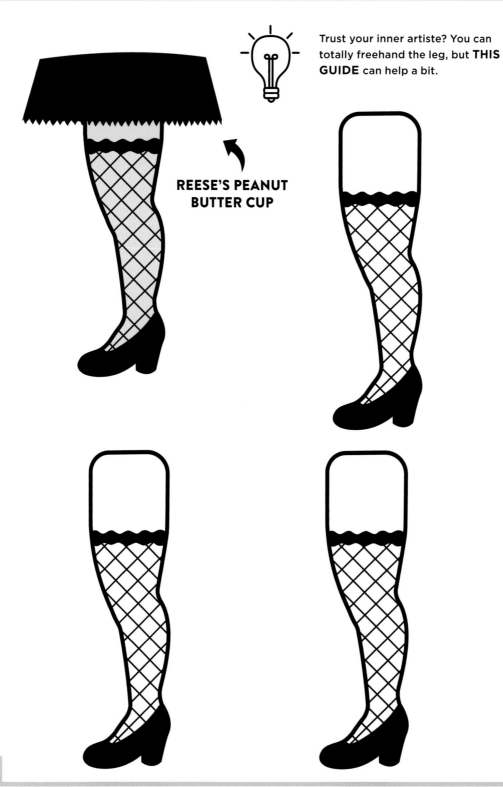

Trust your inner artiste? You can totally freehand the leg, but **THIS GUIDE** can help a bit.

REESE'S PEANUT BUTTER CUP

SHORTBREAD BITES

TOTAL TIME: 45 MIN / MAKES 120

We all like to keep a jar of these around during the holidays—and end up eating our weight in them in no time; it's a little *too* easy to down them by the handful. Plus, you can whip up a batch of these way faster than sugar cookies.

1¼ cups all-purpose flour

3 tablespoons powdered sugar

¼ teaspoon kosher salt

½ teaspoon pure vanilla extract

½ cup (1 stick) butter, softened

1 tablespoon red and green nonpareils or sprinkles

1. Preheat oven to 325°F.

2. In a food processor, pulse flour, powdered sugar, salt, vanilla, and butter until combined. Transfer dough to a large bowl and knead until it comes together. Add nonpareils and knead until combined.

3. Transfer dough to parchment paper and roll into a ½-inch-thick square. Freeze 15 minutes.

4. Cut dough into ½-inch squares and transfer to a large baking sheet. Bake until cookies are golden, 18 to 20 minutes. Let cool on pans.

 Make these any time of year by swapping out the red and green nonpareils for **RAINBOW SPRINKLES**.

INSANELY SOFT GINGER-MOLASSES COOKIES

TOTAL TIME: 1 HR 30 MIN / MAKES 24

Not your average ginger cookie: With a sharp, spicy flavor and ridiculously pillowy texture, these always make our Christmas list.

2 cups all-purpose flour

1¼ teaspoons baking soda

½ teaspoon baking powder

2 teaspoons ground ginger

1½ teaspoons ground cinnamon

½ teaspoon freshly ground black pepper

¼ teaspoon ground cloves

1 teaspoon kosher salt

¾ cup (1½ sticks) butter, softened

½ cup packed brown sugar

⅓ cup molasses

1 large egg

1 teaspoon pure vanilla extract

1 tablespoon grated fresh ginger

¼ cup granulated sugar

1. Preheat oven to 350°F and line two large baking sheets with parchment paper.

2. In a medium bowl, whisk together flour, baking soda, baking powder, ground ginger, cinnamon, pepper, cloves, and salt.

3. In a large bowl using a hand mixer, beat butter and brown sugar until light and fluffy. Add molasses, egg, vanilla, and fresh ginger and beat until incorporated. Add dry ingredients to wet ingredients and beat until just combined. Cover and refrigerate at least 1 hour.

4. Using a medium cookie scoop, roll dough into 1½-inch balls. Roll in granulated sugar and place on prepared baking sheets, spacing cookies 2 inches apart.

5. Bake until puffed and golden around edges, about 10 minutes.

HOT CHOCOLATE BROWNIE CUPS

TOTAL TIME: 50 MIN / MAKES 12

The holiday party trick that will make everyone say "Cuuuuuutteeee!" Creating a "handle" with a broken piece of chocolate-covered pretzel is one of our proudest moments.

Cooking spray

1 (18.3-ounce) box brownie mix, plus ingredients called for on box

1 cup mini marshmallows

⅓ cup semisweet chocolate chips

1 tablespoon coconut oil

1 cup chocolate-covered pretzels

Red, green, and white nonpareils

1. Preheat oven to 350°F and grease a muffin tin with cooking spray.

2. Prepare brownie batter according to package instructions. Fill prepared muffin cups three-quarters full with batter. Bake until edges are set but centers look a little undercooked, 12 to 15 minutes.

3. Press mini marshmallows into centers of brownie cups and return to oven. Bake until marshmallows puff and melt, 3 to 5 minutes. Let cups cool in pan 15 to 20 minutes, then transfer to a wire rack to cool completely.

4. In a heatproof bowl, microwave chocolate chips until melted, then stir in coconut oil. Break off pieces of chocolate-covered pretzels and use melted chocolate to stick them to sides of cookie cups to create handles. Let set.

5. Drizzle remaining melted chocolate over marshmallows and top with sprinkles before serving.

ANDES CHIP COOKIES

TOTAL TIME: 25 MIN / MAKES 38

We look for any excuse to bake with Andes mints. The espresso powder is optional here, but it makes the cookie taste like a peppermint latte, so skip it with caution. Melted butter in the batter = a wayyy fudgier cookie.

3 cups all-purpose flour

1½ teaspoons baking soda

1 teaspoon espresso powder (optional)

½ teaspoon kosher salt

1 cup (2 sticks) melted butter

1 cup packed brown sugar

½ cup granulated sugar

2 large eggs

1 teaspoon pure vanilla extract

1 cup chopped Andes mints

1 cup semisweet chocolate chips

1. Preheat oven to 375°F and line two large baking sheets with parchment paper.

2. In a medium bowl, whisk together flour, baking soda, espresso powder (if using), and salt until combined.

3. In a large bowl using a hand mixer, beat melted butter and sugars until smooth. Add eggs, one at a time, and beat until incorporated, then add vanilla. Gradually add dry ingredients to wet ingredients and beat until just combined. Fold in most of the Andes mints and chocolate chips (reserve some for pressing on tops of cookies).

4. Using a medium cookie scoop, form dough into balls (about 1½ inches) and place on prepared baking sheets, spacing cookies 2 inches apart. Flatten slightly, then top with remaining Andes and chocolate chips.

5. Bake until set and edges are golden, 10 to 12 minutes.

FRENCH BROAD CHOCOLATE LOUNGE

ASHEVILLE, N.C.

IN 2003, Jael Rattigan had her come-to-chocolate moment. "I was in business school at the time and had that late-twenties lost feeling," she starts. "I was hand-rolling truffles in dark chocolate—I made them for friends and family—and my hands were covered, and I felt this tingling sensation. I looked down and just said out loud, 'Chocolate is the thing that will make me happy.'" And it has.

Jael and her husband, Dan, landed in Asheville, N.C., by way of Costa Rica, where they spent two years learning about cacao. After selling bonbons, truffles, and brownies at farmers markets for a year, the pair opened French Broad

Chocolate Lounge in 2008. There, they expanded their menu of confections and pastries—and the Chocolate Snickerdoodle was born.

"It's kind of like if a brownie and a cookie had a baby," Jael laughs, trying to describe it. "It's fudgy, with a deep cocoa flavor and a hint of warmth from the cinnamon." Its unconventional ingredients—safflower oil, coconut milk, maple syrup—make it vegan, but they don't alter the taste. Customers are obsessed. "It's a humble cookie," Jael says. "You've got that subtle chocolate crackle and crunchy sugar topping."

FRENCH BROAD CHOCOLATE LOUNGE'S

CHOCOLATE SNICKERDOODLES

TOTAL TIME: 45 MIN / MAKES 16

1¾ cups granulated sugar

1 cup safflower oil

⅔ cup coconut milk

½ cup maple syrup

1 tablespoon plus 1 teaspoon pure vanilla extract

3½ cups all-purpose flour

1¼ cups unsweetened cocoa powder

1½ teaspoons baking soda

1 teaspoon kosher salt

2 teaspoons ground cinnamon, divided

¾ cup Demerara sugar

1. Preheat oven to 400°F and line two large baking sheets with parchment paper.

2. In a large bowl, whisk together sugar, oil, coconut milk, maple syrup, and vanilla.

3. In a medium bowl, whisk together flour, cocoa powder, baking soda, salt, and 1 teaspoon of cinnamon. Sift dry ingredients over wet ingredients, then fold together with a rubber spatula, scraping sides and bottom of bowl.

4. In a small bowl, whisk together Demerara sugar and remaining 1 teaspoon cinnamon. Using an extra-large cookie scoop (about ¼ cup), scoop dough, then roll into balls and roll in cinnamon-sugar. Transfer dough to prepared baking sheets, spacing cookies 2 inches apart, and flatten slightly.

5. Bake until cookies begin to crack, 8 minutes. Repeat with remaining dough.

PECAN PIE BROWNIES

TOTAL TIME: 1 HR 25 MIN / MAKES 24

Craving all the flavors of pecan pie but not in the mood to labor over one? This brownie hack will get you your fix. You bake up a box, then slather on a syrupy topping of maple syrup, brown sugar, butter, and pecans. Don't sleep on these the rest of the year.

Cooking spray

1 (18.3-ounce) box brownie mix, plus ingredients called for on box

¾ cup packed brown sugar

4 tablespoons (½ stick) melted butter

⅓ cup maple syrup

2 teaspoons pure vanilla extract

½ teaspoon kosher salt

2 large eggs

3½ cups whole or chopped pecans

1. Preheat oven to 350°F. Line a 9×13-inch pan with parchment paper and grease with cooking spray.

2. Prepare brownie batter according to package instructions and pour into prepared pan. Bake until a toothpick inserted into the center comes out with a few moist crumbs, about 20 minutes.

3. In a medium bowl, whisk together brown sugar, melted butter, maple syrup, vanilla, and salt until smooth. Add eggs, one at a time, and whisk until incorporated, then add pecans. Stir until fully coated.

4. Top baked brownies with pecan topping, spreading it evenly. Return to oven and bake until pecan mixture is set, 20 minutes more. Let cool completely before slicing into squares and serving.

Make these **BOOZY** by adding 3 tablespoons rum or bourbon and an additional 2 tablespoons all-purpose flour to the cheesecake batter.

MINI EGGNOG CHEESECAKES

TOTAL TIME: 3 HR 30 MIN / MAKES 16

This crust hack is gold: All you have to do is place a gingersnap cookie in your cupcake liner, pour over the batter, and done.

---

16 gingersnap cookies

2 (8-ounce) blocks cream cheese, softened

½ cup granulated sugar

⅓ cup eggnog

2 large eggs

1 teaspoon pure vanilla extract

1½ tablespoons all-purpose flour

1 teaspoon ground nutmeg

1 teaspoon ground cinnamon

Pinch kosher salt

Whipped cream, for serving

Caramel, for serving

1. Preheat oven to 350°F and line two muffin tins with 16 cupcake liners. Place a gingersnap cookie at the bottom of each lined muffin cup.

2. In a large bowl using a hand mixer, beat cream cheese and sugar until fluffy. Add eggnog and vanilla and beat until incorporated. Add eggs, one at a time, and beat until incorporated, then add flour, nutmeg, cinnamon, and salt.

3. Spoon cheesecake mixture into muffin cups over gingersnaps and bake until set but centers are still slightly jiggly, about 20 minutes. Refrigerate until chilled, about 3 hours and up to overnight.

4. Remove cheesecakes from muffin tins and peel off paper liners. Dollop each cheesecake with whipped cream and drizzle with caramel before serving.

CHRISTMAS LIGHT CUPCAKES

TOTAL TIME: 1 HR 30 MIN / MAKES 18

A baking hack you def need to remember: Mini M&Ms make the most clever string of Christmas lights. These will win every holiday sweets swap.

FOR THE CUPCAKES

1¾ cups all-purpose flour

1¾ cups granulated sugar

¾ cup unsweetened cocoa powder

1 teaspoon baking powder

½ teaspoon baking soda

1 teaspoon kosher salt

1 cup buttermilk

½ cup vegetable oil

2 large eggs

1 teaspoon pure vanilla extract

1 cup boiling water

FOR THE FROSTING

1½ cups heavy cream

1 (8-ounce) block cream cheese, softened

1 cup sugar

1 teaspoon pure vanilla extract

¼ teaspoon kosher salt

FOR DECORATING

Black decorating gel

Mini M&Ms

1. Make cupcakes: Preheat oven to 350°F and line two muffin tins with 18 cupcake liners.

2. In a large bowl, whisk together flour, sugar, cocoa powder, baking powder, baking soda, and salt. Add buttermilk, oil, eggs, and vanilla and stir until incorporated. Add boiling water and mix until just combined.

3. Fill cupcake liners three-quarters full with batter and bake until a toothpick inserted into center of each cupcake comes out clean, 20 minutes. Let cool in pans 5 to 10 minutes, then transfer to a wire rack to cool completely.

4. Make frosting: In a large bowl using a hand mixer, beat heavy cream until stiff peaks form.

5. In another large bowl using a hand mixer, beat cream cheese, sugar, vanilla, and salt until light and fluffy. Gently fold in whipped cream. Transfer to a piping bag fit with a large round tip.

6. Pipe frosting onto cooled cupcakes, giving them height. Using black decorating gel, trace a line around the frosting, then dot the line with mini M&Ms, imitating a string of holiday lights.

SWEET POTATO PIE CUPCAKES

TOTAL TIME: 1 HR 30 MIN / MAKES 12

This cupcake batter has an entire can of sweet potato puree. Keep on telling yourself that while you try everything possible to stop snacking on the marshmallow frosting.

FOR THE GRAHAM CRACKER CRUST

1 cup crushed graham crackers

4 tablespoons (½ stick) melted butter

2 teaspoons granulated sugar

FOR THE CUPCAKES

1 (15-ounce) box yellow cake mix

1 (15-ounce) can sweet potato puree

½ teaspoon ground cinnamon

¼ teaspoon ground nutmeg

Marshmallow Frosting

Chopped toasted pecans, for garnish

Cinnamon-sugar, for garnish

1. Preheat oven to 350°F and line a muffin tin with cupcake liners.

2. Make crust: In a medium bowl, stir together graham cracker crumbs, melted butter, and sugar. Press 1 tablespoon of mixture into bottom of each cupcake liner.

3. Make cupcakes: In a large bowl using a hand mixer, beat cake mix, sweet potato puree, cinnamon, and nutmeg until combined. Pour batter into prepared muffin tin cups, filling them three-quarters full.

4. Bake until golden and a toothpick inserted into center of each cupcake comes out clean, about 22 minutes. Let cool completely.

5. Transfer frosting to a piping bag fitted with a large closed star tip.

6. Pipe frosting onto cooled cupcakes. Garnish with pecans and cinnamon-sugar before serving.

MARSHMALLOW FROSTING

Beat 1 cup softened **BUTTER** with 1 (7.5-ounce) container **MARSHMALLOW CREME** until fluffy. Add 1½ cups **POWDERED SUGAR**, 1 teaspoon pure **VANILLA EXTRACT,** and a pinch of **KOSHER SALT** until smooth.

CHRISTMAS BLONDIES

TOTAL TIME: 40 MIN / SERVES 9

When you wanna be naughty and not nice, make these. Each square is loaded with crushed Oreos, M&Ms, and chocolate chips. Go really wild and swap in white chocolate chips for half the semisweet ones.

Cooking spray

2 cups all-purpose flour

¾ teaspoon baking powder

½ teaspoon kosher salt

¾ cup (1½ sticks) butter, softened

1 cup granulated sugar

½ cup packed brown sugar

2 large eggs

2 teaspoons pure vanilla extract

8 Oreos, crushed

½ cup red and green M&Ms

½ cup semisweet chocolate chips

1. Preheat oven to 350°F and grease a 9×9-inch pan with cooking spray.

2. In a medium bowl, whisk together flour, baking powder, and salt.

3. In a large bowl using a hand mixer, beat butter and sugars until light and fluffy. Add eggs, one at a time, and beat until incorporated, then add vanilla. Add dry ingredients to wet ingredients and beat until just combined. Fold in Oreos, M&Ms, and chocolate chips.

4. Press batter into prepared pan and bake until golden and still slightly soft in the middle, 25 to 30 minutes. Let cool completely before slicing into squares and serving.

CREDITS

FRONT COVER PHOTOGRAPHY
Nigel Cox

COVER FOOD STYLING
Micah Morton

COVER ART DIRECTION
Jessica Musumeci

INTERIOR PHOTOGRAPHY
Parker Feierbach
Ethan Calabrese
Allie Holloway
Lindsay Conchar
Delish Team: 8-9
Courtesy of Macaron Parlour: 56
Courtesy of Strahan & Sara: 71
Courtesy of Do: 184
Nate Webster for French Broad Chocolate: 218

PHOTO EDITOR
Christina Creutz

JOANNA SALTZ HEADSHOTS
Danielle Daly

ANOTHER HUGE THANK YOU . . .

To the incredible Delish team, including **Lindsey Ramsey**, **Lindsay Funston**, **Lauren Miyashiro**, **Sarah Weinberg**, **Lena Abraham**, **Makinze Gore**, **June Xie**, **Tess Koman**, and **Julia Smith**; to our visual guideposts **Nicolas Neubeck**, **Allie Folino**, and **Jessica Musumeci**; to our mentors at Hearst, including **Kate Lewis**, **Troy Young**, **Jacqueline Deval**, and **Brian Madden**; to our friends and partners at **Houghton Mifflin Harcourt**, including **Justin Schwartz**, **Marina Padakis Lowry**, and **Allison Chi**; and to my incredible family, **Scott**, **Spencer**, **Teddy**, and **Everett**, who inspire me to be (and bake) something better every day.

INDEX

Note: Page references in *italics* refer to photos.